Participatory Archives in a World of Ubiquitous Media

The media environment of today is characterised by two critical factors: the development and adoption of ubiquitous mobile devices, and the strengthening of connectivity enabled by advances in ICT infrastructure and social media platforms. These developments have mediated interactions and relationships between citizens and cultural custodians, as well as the ways archives are developed, kept and used. Archives are now characterised by greater socialisations and networks that actively contribute to the signification of cultural heritage value. A range of new stakeholders, many of whom include the public, have sought to define what needs to be collectively remembered and forgotten. The world in which one or a few professional archivists worked on the sole mission of shaping how a society remembers is being displaced by a more democratised culture and the new generation of digitally networked archivists that are its natives. Using a range of case studies and perspectives, this book provides insights to the many ways that ubiquitous media have influenced archival practices and research, as well as the social and civic consequences of present-day archives.

This book was published as a special issue of *Archives and Manuscripts*.

Natalie Pang is an Assistant Professor at the School of Communication and Information, Nanyang Technological University. Her primary research interest is in participatory archives and civic engagement, and information behaviour in contexts of new media and crises.

Kai Khiun Liew is an Assistant Professor at the Wee Kim Wee School of Communication and Information at the Nanyang Technological University. His research interests include Popular Culture Studies, Cultural Memories and Heritage Studies.

Brenda Chan is an independent scholar with research interests in the relationships between new media, heritage and memories.

Participatory Archives in a World of Ubiquitous Media

Edited by

Natalie Pang, Kai Khiun Liew and Brenda Chan

LONDON AND NEW YORK

First published 2015
by Routledge

2 Park Square, Milton Park, Abingdon, Oxon OX14 4RN
711 Third Avenue, New York, NY 10017, USA

Routledge is an imprint of the Taylor & Francis Group, an informa business

First issued in paperback 2017

British Library Cataloguing in Publication Data
A catalogue record for this book is available from the British Library

ISBN13: 978-1-138-89102-9 (hbk)
ISBN13: 978-1-138-05984-9 (pbk)

Typeset in Times New Roman
by RefineCatch Limited, Bungay, Suffolk

Publisher's Note
The publisher accepts responsibility for any inconsistencies that may have arisen during the conversion of this book from journal articles to book chapters, namely the possible inclusion of journal terminology.

Contents

Citation Information

The chapters in this book were originally published in *Archives and Manuscripts*, volume 42, issue 1 (March 2014). When citing this material, please use the original page numbering for each article, as follows:

Chapter 1
Participatory archives in a world of ubiquitous media
Natalie Pang, Kai Khiun Liew and Brenda Chan
Archives and Manuscripts, volume 42, issue 1 (March 2014) pp. 1–4

Chapter 2
Designing dynamic descriptive frameworks
Joanne Evans
Archives and Manuscripts, volume 42, issue 1 (March 2014) pp. 5–18

Chapter 3
Keepers of Ghosts: old signs, new media and the age of archival flux
Lisa Cianci and Stefan Schutt
Archives and Manuscripts, volume 42, issue 1 (March 2014) pp. 19–32

Chapter 4
Convergence, connectivity, ephemeral and performed: new characteristics of digital photographs
Jessica Bushey
Archives and Manuscripts, volume 42, issue 1 (March 2014) pp. 33–47

Chapter 5
Visualising Famagusta: interdisciplinary approaches to the study of the Orthodox Cathedral of Saint George of the Greeks in Famagusta, Cyprus
Sven J Norris, Michael JK Walsh and Thomas A Kaffenberger
Archives and Manuscripts, volume 42, issue 1 (March 2014) pp. 48–60

Chapter 6
Digital archives and metadata as critical infrastructure to keep community memory safe for the future – lessons from Japanese activities
Shigeo Sugimoto
Archives and Manuscripts, volume 42, issue 1 (March 2014) pp. 61–72

Chapter 7

Collecting the easily missed stories: digital participatory microhistory and the South Asian American Digital Archive
Michelle Caswell and Samip Mallick
Archives and Manuscripts, volume 42, issue 1 (March 2014) pp. 73–86

Chapter 8

Archiving the wild, the wild archivist: Bukit Brown Cemetery and Singapore's emerging 'docu-tivists'
Natalie Pang and Liew Kai Khiun
Archives and Manuscripts, volume 42, issue 1 (March 2014) pp. 87–97

Please direct any queries you may have about the citations to clsuk.permissions@cengage.com

Participatory archives in a world of ubiquitous media

Natalie Pang, Kai Khiun Liew and Brenda Chan

> I dream of a new age of curiosity. We have the technical means for it; the desire is there; the things to be known are infinite; the people who can employ themselves at this task exist. Why do we suffer? From too little: from channels that are too narrow, skimpy, quasi-monopolistic, insufficient. There is no point in adopting a protectionist attitude, to prevent 'bad' information from invading and suffocating the 'good'. Rather, we must multiply the paths and the possibility of comings and goings.[1]

Many archivists in the past few decades have reassessed many of their core beliefs, challenging the positivism that was entrenched in professional thinking which favoured objectivity, detachment, authenticity and truth. In the wake of this reassessment, which in many other disciplines became associated with the label 'postmodernity', archivists have learnt to embrace diversity, subjective values and participatory principles. These developments have been fostered through scholarly dialogues within the archiving community, among users of archives, as well as through the impact of the contemporary media environment.

Today's media is characterised by two critical factors: the development and adoption of ubiquitous mobile devices, and the strengthening of connectivity enabled by advances in ICT infrastructure and social media platforms. These developments have intensified the mediation of social relationships and interactions, bringing about a media environment that is more than the information being created or used, and more than just tools or platforms for communication. As van Dijck has explained, we are now in a culture of connectivity arising from technological innovations that have been instrumental in blurring the boundaries between the private and public throughout our contemporary existence, and no less so within archival cultures.[2]

With the introduction of social media in the early 2000s, archives have gone beyond being merely physical or digital entities; they are now also characterised by greater socialisations and networks that actively contribute to the signification of cultural heritage value. A range of new stakeholders, many of whom include the public, have sought to define what needs to be collectively remembered and forgotten. The world in which one or a few professional archivists worked on the sole mission of shaping how a society remembers is being displaced by a more democratised culture and the new generation of digitally networked archivists that are its natives.

Such explorations of new media demonstrate the democratic potential of contemporary archives, reflecting the 'new age of curiosity' referred to by Michel Foucault in an interview published in 1980.[3] The technical means now present in the contemporary media environment, coupled with the present-day imaginations and expertise of social actors, have given rise to the construction of new forms of memories characterised by cooperative remembrance and recursive reflections integrated as part of everyday practices. As Schwartz and Cook have pointed out, there is power in archives as they shape what is remembered about the past as well as what becomes of significance in the present and the future.[4] The shift of archival practices and privileges from institutions to individuals underlies the changing power relations of contemporary archival cultures in persuading and mobilising, creating awareness and exerting influence on various social actors and political powers in society.

The possibilities are exciting, but challenges abound as fundamental and practical questions are raised about the archivist's role(s), existing practices and how to deal with the chaos of 'wild' archives popping up everywhere and the lack of structured metadata. The need to reconsider which contemporary archives need to be managed (or not managed), and how this will be achieved, is a primary occupation of the archivist today.

This special issue of *Archives and Manuscripts* is timely as we reflect on what it means for archiving in today's media environment, given the growing complexities brought about by technological innovations and broader social changes. Moving from the predominant preoccupation to institutionalise the keeping of records chronologically as history, archivists are becoming cognisant of the increasingly individualised and democratised processes and acts of collective remembering involved in producing and reproducing records as memories.[5]

The papers

The papers in this special issue straddle a continuum of new media possibilities. On one hand new types of records and interactions may be created, and on the other, new media offer opportunities to revitalise and 'save' records that are at risk of being destroyed and forgotten. In between, there are various possibilities in which new media mediate the keeping of records in archives.

Some of the papers here were originally presented at an international conference on 'New Media, Memories and Histories', which took place on 5–6 October 2012 at the Wee Kim Wee School of Communication and Information, Nanyang Technological University, Singapore. The conference brought together scholars from leading research institutions in the United Kingdom, Australia, Taiwan, Japan, Singapore, the Philippines, Israel and Yugoslavia, all of whom have been working on various forms of contemporary archives. Out of the 19 papers presented at the conference, five have been included in the final selection here because they addressed issues that would shape the conceptual definitions and impact of archives. After the open call for papers, more papers were received and the resulting seven papers were selected and revised to align with the tighter focus of the special issue.

The special issue begins with Joanne Evans's autoethnographical examination of her experience as an archival systems designer and developer in Australia for 15 years beginning in 1995. Reflections on archiving within contemporary paradigms are synthesised through her journey of involvements in a series of archives projects. The projects are also symbolic of the phases of technological development on the Web, and the evolution and development of archives standards. Her experiences and the developments of the projects are thus also a story of how the archives profession, at least in the Australian context, has reached where it is today, and the challenges as well as opportunities to be confronted.

Related stories are retold and new lessons discovered in Lisa Cianci and Stefan Schutt's discussion of the Keepers of Ghosts project, in which digital images of old painted signboards from Melbourne are revived, remembered and reconstructed in an online archive characterised by the participation of multiple stakeholders: residents, café owners, enthusiasts, researchers, artists.

The opportunities and challenges of digital photographs, records that are commonly found in contemporary archives, are discussed by Jessica Bushey as she argues for their convergence, connectivity, ephemeralness and performativity. The paper highlights the need to confront issues such as value and trustworthiness when keeping and managing archives containing digital photographs.

The rich possibilities of new media are highlighted in the interdisciplinary and collaborative work of Sven Norris, Michael Walsh and Thomas Kaffenberger. In their digital reconstruction of the historic walled city of Famagusta from Cyprus, they raise questions about how new community memories may be mediated, their sociopolitical implications and how reconciliation may be achieved through the multimedia archive.

In the work of another contested site, Natalie Pang and Liew Kai Khiun reflect on how a documentation and archiving team and 'docu-tivists' may come together using digital and participatory technologies to shape the meanings and what is to be remembered about Bukit Brown Cemetery in Singapore. The site has been marked for partial removal for a highway and, subsequently, the planned clearance of the site for residential projects. The participatory archive mediates meanings and perceived heritage value, but also shapes relationships and connections within and between interest groups and the state.

The disasters facing the world today make up a significant part of the external transformations contemporary archives have to deal with. On this note, Shigeo Sugimoto shares his experiences in digital archives initiatives in Japan, where insights and archives have been shaped by the Japanese earthquake of 2011. Focusing on the importance of digital archives for long-term longevity of community memories as resilience against disasters, he also suggests how digital archives may be developed as a platform for communities to actively participate in collective acts of remembering.

In their research on the South Asian American Digital Archive, Michelle Caswell and Samip Mallick expound on how archivists participate and govern the First Days Project, a project showcasing stories of South Asian immigrants' first days in the United States in various forms: text, audio and video. New grounds and practices as archivists are being found and redefined, as the authors also reflect on the modern-day functions fulfilled by the participatory project.

Aspirations and realities

All of the papers in this issue are underlined by the common motivation to provide new conceptual frameworks and ideas whilst examining archives in the contemporary media environment. Read as a whole, it should serve to provide novel perspectives on the various forms of archives being constructed, preserved and sustained by the highly circulatory networks of new media.

The power and potential of archives in helping communities and stakeholders to navigate through present disasters, political instabilities and threats of disappearance is also evident in the way the authors in this issue make observations about the extended functions of archives, and their impacts on the state and society.

Such potential, not always realised in every project, suggests that the aspirations of contemporary archives are also punctuated by realities such as lack of funding, conservative definitions in the scope of archiving and inadequate access to technologies, as well as negotiations of power between community stakeholders, researchers and the state. It does imply that the work of the contemporary archivist and archives is much more indeterminate and challenging.

Endnotes

1. M Foucault, 'The Masked Philosopher', in *Michael Foucault: Politics, Philosophy, Culture, Interviews and Other Writings 1977–1984,* LD Kritzman (ed.), Routledge, London, 1988, pp. 198–99.
2. J van Dijck, *The Culture of Connectivity: A Critical History of Social Media*, Oxford University Press, Oxford, 2013.
3. Foucault, pp. 189–199. Interestingly, Foucault made these comments at the same time that Tim Berners-Lee, working at CERN, had started to develop the technology that a little over 10 years later would mature into the World Wide Web.
4. J Schwartz and T Cook, 'Archives, Records and Power: The Making of Modern Memory', *Archival Science*, vol. 2, nos 1–2, 2002, pp. 1–19.
5. J O'Toole and R Cox, *Understanding Archives and Manuscripts*, Society of American Archivists, Chicago, 2006.

Designing dynamic descriptive frameworks

Joanne Evans

Dr Joanne Evans is a lecturer in the Faculty of Information Technology, Monash University, and coordinator of the Records Continuum Research Group, part of the Faculty's Centre of Organisational and Social Informatics. She has many years of experience in archival systems development, with the technologies she has been involved in designing and developing deployed into a number of research projects, as well as being utilised in small archives settings. Joanne undertook her PhD at Monash as part of the Australian Research Council Linkage-funded Clever Recordkeeping Metadata Project (2003–06) and received a Vice Chancellor's Commendation for Doctoral Thesis Excellence for her thesis, Building Capacities for Sustainable Recordkeeping Metadata Interoperability. Her research interests lie in the multifarious roles metadata plays in creating, managing and sustaining information and recordkeeping infrastructure and systems, with an increasing emphasis on the nature of archival design.

Cultural heritage professionals use descriptive metadata as a tool to manage and mediate access to the memory texts in their custody. With digital and networking technologies exploding the possibilities for capturing recorded memories and memorialising lives, loves and losses, they can, and should, revolutionise our recordkeeping metadata management frameworks. Embracing the 'archival turn' requires relinquishing our role as the dominant descriptive storyteller, but are our current descriptive models and systems a barrier rather than a facilitator of such a transformation? In this paper the author adopts an autoethnographical approach to explore her experience of developing archival systems since the advent of the Web in the mid-1990s. The story involves a range of metadata schemas and models, questioning their ability to enable the design of interfaces to recorded knowledge and memories that tap into and unleash the dynamic capabilities of the new technologies and their potential to reflect a multiplicity of voices. The paper will contribute to the growing body of literature about the role of archival professionals in shaping recorded memory through their standards and practices, challenging our image as merely silent partners and neutral players.

Introduction

Many archivists are all too aware of the enormity of the challenges facing the profession in this digital and networked information age. In two decades rapid evolution of Web and other information and communication technologies have transformed the Internet into a ubiquitous, pervasive, information infrastructure, embedded in our working, social, public and private lives. It has exploded the possibilities for capturing recorded memories, tracking activities and memorialising lives. Discussion and debate of our role in this new paradigm, of the sustainability and scalability of our systems and processes, and of the conceptualisations that do, and do not, help us make sense of this new landscape characterise the professional and scholarly literature.[1] In a pre-Internet world we could get away with the automation of paper-based records and archives management practices. But now understanding, harnessing and exploiting the capabilities of digital and networking technologies for archival and recordkeeping endeavours in a myriad of contexts – some old, mature and traditional, others new, emergent and transformational – is our grand challenge.[2] The design and development of frameworks, standards and tools for representing and managing recordkeeping metadata to address complexity and pluralisation in the context of a growing participatory archives movement is a key part of this agenda.[3]

Design challenges for archival descriptive frameworks

Recordkeeping metadata are the layers of structured information which tie recorded information objects to the contexts in which they are created, managed and used, so that they may function as authentic and reliable evidence of those activities.[4] Records do not exist without recordkeeping metadata, whether it is implicit, explicit, intrinsic or extrinsic. It enables records to be discoverable, accessible and interpretable, formulating and structuring evidential and memory management frameworks. Records are networked information objects, bound in webs of evidentiary and contextual relationships.[5] We now have digital and networking technologies to fully exploit this characteristic.

Traditional archival description practices have relied on recordkeeping metadata inscribed on physical records, reflected in their arrangement and documented in current recordkeeping tools.[6] They involve re-creating and augmenting it through archiving processes, making business and recordkeeping contexts explicit as records are removed from their originating environment and transferred to an archive.[7] Archivists have then made this metadata available in a variety of forms, for example, through finding aids, catalogues, indexes and registers, to facilitate discovery, access and further use of the records.

From a records continuum perspective this is but one way in which description, a 'complex multi-layered recordkeeping function' which creates, captures, organises and pluralises recordkeeping metadata, may be enacted.[8] Layers of recordkeeping metadata capture and tell past and ongoing stories of the records,[9] and as records themselves, are also 'always in the process of becoming'.[10] Rather than just supporting static cataloguing and freezing records in archival stasis, our descriptive frameworks need to facilitate capture of dynamic webs of transactions and relationships to document 'juridical-administrative, provenancial, procedural, documentary and technological contexts' of creation, management and use.[11]

The nature, availability and accessibility of recordkeeping metadata impacts what is remembered, how it is remembered and what gets forgotten.[12] Heather MacNeil calls for archivists to look into 'surrendering our role as invisible and omniscient narrators and accepting that we are among the characters in the story told through our descriptions' and so need 'to render an account of our role and responsibility in the process of our representation'.[13] She also advocates for transforming practices to capitalise on networking capabilities of new information technologies:

> The Web is an ideal vehicle for transcending the artificial limits imposed by current descriptive practices and for exploiting an expanded vision of archival description; one that unseats the privileged status currently accorded to the standards-based finding aid and repositions it as a complex network of hyperlinked and interactive documentation relating to

> the history, appraisal, preservation, use and interpretation of a body of records over time. Such a network could provide users with multiple pathways to explore, which the user would be free to pursue or ignore. It could also provide users with the opportunity to create new pathways by incorporating spaces in which users are free to contribute additional perspectives and alternate readings on the records and their representations.[14]

Can our existing descriptive infrastructure support this vision? Are we able to just tack it on to what we currently do? Or does it require a more extensive transformation? Other communities, primarily in information discovery spaces, are using semantic web technologies to create networks of description around information resources.[15] Can we adopt what they are doing? Are these technologies and networks archival? If not, what adaptions are needed to encompass archival dimensions and support intergenerational transmission of evidence and memory?

Responding to these calls to transform our descriptive frameworks requires understanding, not just of particular technologies, systems and requirements, but of design itself. Designing is a multi-faceted, recursive, iterative and reflexive process which transforms an idea into some kind of material form, to make a useful difference to the situation or task at hand.[16] It is a complex, structured, creative, problem-solving activity in which prior understandings are built upon, developed and transformed as conceptualisations materialise. Good design transports us to a better place, while poor design frustrates and obstructs. A key research question is, what designing skills and knowledge do we need to facilitate networks of archival descriptive systems?

Autoethnographical approach

To investigate this question, I have adopted an autoethnographical approach to examine my experience as an archival systems designer and developer. Over a 15-year period I have been responsible for designing and deploying database software to document and manage records and facilitate their discovery, access and use. With hindsight it can be viewed as an action research process in which 'exploration of the interface between theory and practice' and 'interplay[s] with technology' have been explored through a variety of projects.[17] Iterative and reflexive design of archival database systems has been a method in which I have explored the informatics of recordkeeping and archival systems, and come to a better understanding of the nature and needs of recordkeeping metadata.

While the systems I have designed and developed have been judged from their external presence,[18] I provide here 'an interpretive reading from the inside'[19] and reveal how they are constructs of people, place, time and community as much as technology. Autoethnography is a way of studying my own experience to develop a deeper understanding of the interplay between these constructs in the investigation of designing processes.[20] It also puts my archival practice within the research frame rather than being an invisible and silent force.[21] This extends MacNeil's point about making the role we play in shaping archival description explicit to the information infrastructure we have constructed in support of our practices.

Autoethnography enables me to get inside my archival design processes in order to systematically describe and analyse them as cultural practice.[22] I want to reveal how they have been shaped and influenced by archival doing and thinking, and in turn, through the use that is made of the system, how they then shape and influence archival practice. The aim is for a 'thick' description which sheds insights onto archival design processes, and the design knowledge and skills needed to transform them.

I also want to discuss my particular story of developing archival systems within an Australian context to complement and contrast with those from other contexts.[23] When I started out in the archival profession I took for granted a singular descriptive practice which subsequent international engagement has shown is far from the reality. This raises questions of whether the plurality of archival contexts should be better represented in our international archival description standards rather than their current tendency to assume that a mono-culture is achievable and desirable. This paper is fodder for such a debate.

Designing and developing archival systems

ASAP and the ADS

My story begins in 1995 when I landed my first job with newly minted postgraduate information management qualifications at the Australian Science Archives Project (ASAP). As the 'project' in its name suggests it was not a traditional archival institution. Established in the mid-1980s by historians of Australian science at the University of Melbourne, ASAP's role was to facilitate the transfer of records relating to Australian science, medicine and technology into archival repositories. It was a response to an internationally recognised need to improve the representation and documentation of scientific records in archival collections and to establish appropriate frameworks for their appraisal in the light of the massive expansion in their volume, especially post – World War II.[24] ASAP never intended to become an archival repository; it only ever acted as a temporary store of records for processing on route to the shelves of an appropriate archival institution or back into in-house archives.[25]

The establishment of ASAP coincided with the emergence of a post-custodial discourse in the Australian and international archival community, with the intellectual control over distributed archives, rather than just the caretaking of records in custody, as the focus and scope of archival endeavours.[26] In such a climate, ASAP became a place for exploring the tools and technologies of a post-custodial archival organisation, and part of the Australian community of practice investigating recordkeeping and archiving from a continuum perspective.[27]

To support the processing of records for archival transfer, ASAP invested in database technology and developed the ADS (Archival Data System). It was modelled on the Commonwealth Record Series system, and featured the separate documentation of records, their aggregations, and the organisations and persons associated with their creation and use, and then the programmatic assemblage of these descriptions into finding aids via interrelationships. From this processing tool documentation was generated for the originating creator or custodian of the records, the archival repository that would manage them and for historians and others who would access the records. The database approach enabled descriptive metadata to 'document record content, context, continuity and structure to enable the maintenance of integrity and enhance accessibility' to be captured once and then reproduced in a variety of forms and formats.[28]

The database approach also helped to manage an uncertain and often drawn-out process. It could take many years from initial identifying of records of interest, establishing their scope, securing funding for their processing, carrying out that processing and then, if needed, transferring the records to their new custodian. It also could involve many different players and featured periods of activity and inactivity. ASAP's self-funded status also created a strong desire to develop efficient processes and tools which could be used from one project to another. This focus also meant ASAP was an avid monitor of standard developments in archival and other communities of interest for benchmarking or integrating into the ADS.

The ADS was iteratively developed through a number of processing projects which started small, dealing with the records of individuals and small organisations, and gradually got larger. It culminated in using the system in a series of large processing projects for the records of Generation Victoria, the generation arm of the State Electricity Commission of Victoria, as it was privatised in the mid-1990s. It was the first of these projects that led to my employment at ASAP, initially as the project leader for the first stage of the project and then as the key developer of the ADS as it was migrated to Microsoft Access and its interfaces for management, discovery and access enhanced.[29]

The ADS and the Australian Series System

It was through this process that I was introduced to the Australian literature on archival systems, and the writings of Peter Scott[30] and Chris Hurley[31] in particular. Grappling with data structure and interface design questions, I found their words were of immense practical help as I was introduced to a relational network view of archival description. They enabled me to align ADS development with the Australian Series System Model, while at the same time being aware of where technological and other pragmatics meant concessions. No implementation of the Australian Series System Model is devoid of such compromises. I am well aware of where I have had to bury bones in my systems, hopefully to be remedied at a later stage. As has been pointed out, some of the critique levelled at the model may be more to do with the limitations of any particular implementation rather than deficiencies in the conceptualisation.[32] Designing requires awareness of when practical compromises are a necessity, coupled with the ability to anticipate and judge their consequences.

My enthusiasm for relational database technology and the Australian Series System Model can be seen in a paper prepared for the 1997 Australian Society of Archivists' Conference:

> now the computer technologists have caught up and we have ... the tools to create the system Scott was searching for. With a computer database, the context, record or relationship needs only be documented once. It can then be used in any number of displays – screen, print copy, html and beyond. Fielded information rather than unwieldy slabs of text allow searching and grouping across attributes, so archivists and archives users have a myriad of access points and ways of selecting archival data to satisfy information needs.[33]

It also reflected discussions at ASAP about what we were doing, whether it was effective and how we might better harness the technology to do things smarter and achieve better outcomes. We were encouraged to keep track of what was happening at the cutting edge of information technologies, and to aspire to translate it directly into our processes and systems. Archiving was not about conserving and preserving a staid past, but innovatively securing capabilities into the systems of the future.

One particular area in which we felt we were making a unique contribution to the continuum community of practice was in our processing methodology. Supported by the relational database capabilities of the ADS, we took accessioning to where and when we first came into contact with records, encompassing description of everything sighted, not just that which would subsequently be appraised to have continuing value.[34] MacNeil writes of the 'misleading impression of completeness' as 'a description of a body of records is constructed out of incomplete fragments of evidence'.[35] She suggests we look to the language of archival description to better 'signal to users the gaps in our knowledge'. The ADS experience shows that the language we use in description is only part of the problem. Our processes and data structures need to be designed to capture and represent *all* rather than just part of *our* story in relation to the archival processing of records.

The ADS aimed to support description as a dynamic process. We 'inventory processed' records rather than arranging and describing records. Accessioning would identify initial series and provenance entities but it was through detailed processing of the records that fuller details of relationships to contextual entities were uncovered. It was not about starting with 'fully fledged and finely honed series and provenance descriptions'[36] but allowing for these to emerge in the processing. We often dealt with much-neglected records, remnants of a multitude of recordkeeping systems employed throughout a person's or an organisation's lifetime. Not the relative neatness of government registry systems with documentation of the registry's recordkeeping still extant and accessible.

With the ADS we were not just automating manual descriptive processes but thinking about where technology could enable their refiguring:

> Hence the ADS is not just an automated finding aid. It is an archival management information system. It is a processing tool. It documents records from the time they are identified as part of a records program, through to arrangement and physical location in an archival repository, and beyond to their subsequent use. It brings the many processing and finding aids archivists produce within the one integrated system.[37]

From ADS to HDMS

The completion of the Generation Victoria projects in 1998 brought about a refocusing of ASAP's efforts. It involved going back to working on smaller collections, and with the Web gaining momentum, developing mechanisms for producing HTML finding aids. Organisational change led to ASAP becoming the Australian Science and Technology Heritage Centre (Austehc) and the ADS became the HDMS (Heritage Documentation Management System). The rise of the open source software movement also enabled us to adopt this kind of model for making our system available to others. First-hand knowledge of the effort and expertise that goes into building an archival processing and documentation management system and of the benefits that it could bring made it an imperative.

This and the establishment of Austehc was a statement. We did not want to be software vendors, nor just a history of science project. We were an archival research centre, with modularised, iterative and reflective design, development and deployment of archival systems our methodological focus. Keen to continuously improve the HDMS, we felt that the open source approach could build community capacity, delivering an automation product to the archives community with a minimum of technical barriers, and foster collaborative partnerships for further developments. It could promote efficient and standardised practices, so that smaller archives could more easily gain intellectual and physical control over their records and make this available to users via the Web, participating alongside bigger state and federal government archives and collecting institutions.[38]

We also wanted to remain responsive to practical needs as our experience had shown that the better developments were driven by the demands of real rather than imagined situations. They produced a focused system rather than one overloaded with 'bells and whistles' that someone thought 'might' be useful someday. Along with this was a firm belief in the benefits of modularisation and incremental development rather than attempting to specify a perfect system up-front. The HDMS accrued functionality, demonstrating the benefits of a generic integrated approach rather than producing customised discrete systems. Tailoring came in the way the software was deployed and in the protocols governing archiving processes in particular contexts.

HDMS and EAD

A project with the National Archives of Australia in 1999 gave us the chance to engage with the Encoded Archival Description (EAD) standard. EAD was developed by the US archival community in the mid-1990s as a structured mark-up language to foster web publishing of archival finding aids, catalogues and guides to records.[39] We had built an HTML finding aid generator, and so this project aimed to develop an EAD one, perhaps to replace the HTML one, and through this report on the application of EAD in an Australian Series System context.

Replacing presentational mark-up with structured mark-up was, and still is, highly appealing. With the HTML generation framework in place, re-working to produce EAD was technically pretty straightforward. It took just a few days of programming to develop the 'proof of concept' version. But translating EAD-XML generated output into HTML was a much trickier proposition then than it is today. Browser support of XSL, the style sheet language for translating from XML to HTML, was patchy and browser-specific, and systems to manage the web rendering of XML or SGML documents were expensive.

Aside from these technicalities, the bigger issue was that the data structures of EAD could not adequately represent the rich network of relationships between accession, inventory, series and provenance entity descriptions captured in the HDMS. It only allowed for these to be bundled up into a hierarchy. Moving from HTML to EAD would have involved much more work to achieve a lesser outcome. This work highlighted the difference between the document-based approach to archival description underpinning EAD versus the database approach embodied in the Australian Series System. We concluded that for EAD to be relevant in our context it would need to incorporate appropriate structures for marking up these relationships to represent networks of archival description rather than just hierarchies.[40]

HDMS today

Opportunities to further develop the HDMS since this EAD project have been limited. It still provides the backbone for the archival processing work undertaken by the eScholarship Research Centre, the unit that Austehc has since become, and is also used by a number of archives. As a traditional archival control system, it enables the documentation of records from a singular records creator perspective, with other stakes in records captured within textual descriptions or using indexing mechanisms.[41] Its capacity to deal with a multiplicity of voices is circumscribed by its design, and reflective of the time and place in which it was developed. It has yet to come to terms with evolutions in web technologies and capabilities over the past decade, so while static HTML finding aids can be generated and published, there is no scope for capturing how these are used or for users to add their own perspectives on the records. However, before we can push into this kind of paradigm, we need what the HDMS does deliver – a processing tool to uniquely identify and manage appropriately structured descriptive units and allow for dynamic documentation of their interrelationships.

OHRM and WWW

Early 2000 saw my design focus switch from the HDMS to what became known as the OHRM. This system grew from ASAP's earlier work in establishing a Register of Australian Science Archives (RASA). To play its role in facilitating the transfer of records to archival institutions, ASAP needed to document where records were currently held and where arrangements between scientists and/or their families and archives, museums or libraries already existed. It was clear that this information would be of value beyond ASAP, useful for historians, scientists and archivists in discovering, appraising and using archives of Australian science.[42]

The story of RASA has been told elsewhere,[43] but its design principles need highlighting here. It built from existing work, using Anne Moyal's 1966 *Guide to the Manuscript Records of Australian Science*, re-engineered using relational database technology and an Australian Series System approach. Even though the first publication plan was to produce the register as a book, the database approach was in recognition of the need for an informatic which would allow for its continual updating. Separate database tables documented context, records, custody and the interrelationships between them. Output was generated and published as the *Guide to the Records of the Archives of Science in Australia* in 1991.[44]

With the advent of the World Wide Web in 1994, in Tim Sherratt's hands, RASA became *Bright Sparcs*, incorporating the annual History of Australian Science Bibliography from the *Historical Records of Australian Science*, as well as the *Directory of Archives in Australia* to update and expand the information available about repositories.[45] It re-purposed and re-imagined these paper-based reference tools to take advantage of the capabilities of web technologies. It featured the unique persistent identification of descriptive entities – people, archives, published resources and archival repositories – and then the mapping of relationships between these entities to allow a complex hypertext network to emerge. The Australian Series System Model once again in action.

My role in 2000 was to take the bespoke *Bright Sparcs* database and turn it into a generic system, so others could create their own such network. It was named the Online Heritage Resource Manager (OHRM); a name which it has outgrown although the acronym has stuck. Over a decade later the OHRM has enabled the web publication of a number of contextual knowledge networks, including the *Australian Women's Register*, *Encyclopedia of Australian Science, Australian Dictionary of Biography Online*, *Agreements, Treaties and Negotiated Settlements (ATNS) Database*, *Chinese-Australian Historical Images in Australia (CHIA)* and, most recently, the *Find and Connect Web Resource*.[46] As an archival system, it enables these resources to be built for the long term, which in a digital and networked world implies openness, scalability and interoperability.

With hindsight, I can categorise my development work with the ADS/HDMS as being about learning the informatics of the Australian Series System, whereas with the OHRM it has been about expanding and exploiting it. As the potential of the OHRM unfolded, so too did the philosophy underpinning its design. The aim has been to standardise the back-end system (the relational database) on appropriate archival, scholarly, design, accessibility and usability principles, while customising the front-end system (the hypertext network) on appropriate archival, scholarly, design, accessibility and usability principles. The development of the *Find and Connect Web Resource* was an opportunity to articulate a set of 10 principles 'embedded in the informatics and programming code of the OHRM, the web publication practices and processes, and in the experience and skills of the project team'.[47]

With standards-based as the first of these principles, the OHRM design journey has featured engagement with a number of metadata schemas and standards.[48] In looking to extant metadata schemas and descriptive standards my initial focus was on improving the structure of descriptive entities, but it soon became clear that the OHRM also needed to improve ways to capture, represent and then present the relationships between them. This informed my involvement in working groups for the ISO 23081 Standard for Recordkeeping Metadata, where I was a strong advocate of relationships as first-order entities in the modelling of recordkeeping metadata. If building the OHRM from scratch today I would bring relationships to the forefront in the data model and interfaces. The system features some programmatic kludges in this area resulting from a lack of understanding of their entity status in early development work.[49] It is an imperfect rendering and an example of where studying the OHRM artefact would give you an incomplete picture of what was (or is now) in the mind of its designer.

What I did get right early on was building the capacity for OHRM implementers to define their own relationship and entity types, rather than hard-wiring into the data structures those predominantly used in archival standards. This has allowed implementers to define their own ontology of contextual entities and relationships, within standard structures for resource and entity description based on community needs. This has significantly contributed to the diversity of ways in which the OHRM has been deployed with different resource and entity types having the descriptive focus. For *ATNS* this focus is on agreements, treaties and other negotiated settlements between Australian Indigenous communities and other bodies; for *CHIA* description revolves around photographic images and how they have been portrayed in narratives of Chinese-Australian experience.

OHRM and Web 2.0

As OHRM development unfolded during the 2000s, so too did the Web. Trends towards open, integratable technologies and systems became known as Web 2.0, turning web use from passive consumption to active creation, and releasing the might of network effects.[50] We studied Web 2.0 design principles with interest to see where the OHRM was at, concluding that while a product of the pre-Web 2.0 world, it had Web 2.0 leanings. It can generate a niche site of valuable content for a wide variety of users (the long tail), it is based on citation principles and making content open and accessible (some rights reserved, cooperation over control). Its relational model allows network effects to be exploited in the user experience, with its modularity and iterative content-driven design approach reflective of lightweight services and the notion of the perpetual beta.

Where it has fallen behind is in its architecture of participation. While the OHRM data model allows for citation of resources to enrich entity descriptions, the power to do this is in the hands of the OHRM implementer rather than in the user community. Where OHRM projects have incorporated comments and feedback mechanisms, they currently require moderation and manual translation of user contributions into the system's data structures. While many archival institutions are making forays into this area, there is a need for research into participatory descriptive frameworks, especially around enabling them to be archival rather than ephemeral, and integral to descriptive practices. For the archival community I believe that the design challenges go beyond using Web 2.0 to interact with end users, encompassing how these technologies reshape all of our processes and systems.

Interoperability and OAI-PMH

In 2008, an Australian Research Council Linkage Infrastructure Equipment and Facilities Grant enabled some investigation of a federated information architecture for the *Australian Women's Register*, an OHRM flagship and driver of key innovations since its establishment in 2000.[51] In this project we less successfully investigated community methods for populating the *Register*, but more successfully enabled the harvesting of its content using Encoded Archival Context and the Open Archives Initiative Protocol for Metadata Harvesting (OAI-PMH) into the National Library of Australia's Trove discovery service. It gave a glimmer of how descriptive frameworks could be transformed if metadata exchange was bilateral, with sharing and augmenting rather than continuous manual re-creating. Further research and development is needed to put this technical layer in place and to investigate the impact it then has both on the processes for populating a resource such as the *Register* and on interfaces. This would help further understanding of the information interoperability services that institutional players should be looking to provide to facilitate participatory descriptive networks.

Archival design

How does this exploration and reflection on my experiences in designing and developing archival systems help in identifying the designing skills and knowledge needed to facilitate networks of archival descriptive systems? Firstly it illustrates how design is 'a reflective conversation with the materials of a situation'; a process that not only produces an artefact of some kind, but where the designer learns, through reflecting-in-action and reflecting-on-action, about 'the construction of the problem, the strategies of action, or the model of the phenomena'.[52] This means that there are both explicit and tacit outcomes. In my case the tacit skills and knowledge could be translated into the next project and the next iteration of the system. Also as I was working in a university environment with scholarly communication encouraged, it could be achieved through publication, community engagement and the sharing of the systems through open source licences. This does highlight the importance of a robust professional and scholarly discourse to allow for the stories of and around designs of new archival and recordkeeping technologies to be revealed and shared, along with the technologies themselves. We are at a moment where, as we transition into a digital and networked information age, such sharing of technologies, experience and knowledge is vital.

Telling these stories helps us understand and develop our own informatics – the fundamental nature of the structures and processes of archival and recordkeeping systems – so that appropriate interventions, improvements and transformations can be designed and developed. It is no longer just about building our own systems, but facilitating the embedding and embodiment of archival and recordkeeping capabilities in systems, tools and ways of working with digital stuff in a networked world. Archival design is our concern. While others are designing and building synchronic (in time) information networks for discovery and access, we need to be responsible for designing the diachronic (through time) and evidential capabilities into those networks. I am concerned about a tendency within the archival community to assume others will take care of our design concerns in their software, or alternatively just make do with the data structures and functionality they provide. We must be aware of and able to judge the values and tacit assumptions packed into digital technology, particularly where they are at odds with the needs of recordkeeping and archival systems.

My archival design journey also demonstrates how the designs of our systems are a record of archival processes, practices and contexts, as well as a reflection of archival paradigms. In the case of the HDMS and the OHRM, awareness of the conceptual framework on which they are built is overt, and as I have noted one of my motives in telling this story was to highlight this to enable comparison and contrast with those coming from other descriptive contexts. It also serves to further MacNeil's point – our omniscient narration extends to not just our descriptions but our descriptive systems. Their structure and functionality impacts on what gets remembered, how it gets remembered and the degree to which others can participate in our evidential and memory management frameworks.

My design and development experience is supportive of the need to move away from hierarchical descriptive models and towards networked ones in order to enable greater participation. These have the potential to represent complex and ongoing relationships between people, stories and records, but we have a way to go in opening up our descriptive silos so that they can function as nodes in a participatory network. A key responsibility is how we do this archivally and enable appropriate evidence of these dynamic networks of documentation to be carried forward through time. We need participatory archival design methodologies to foster the development of archival systems configured around community information, self-knowledge and memory needs leading to transformative changes in archival description, access and other recordkeeping services.

Conclusion

The role of archivists in this new descriptive paradigm is to be less involved in crafting archival descriptions and more involved in creating sustainable, scalable and open archival descriptive frameworks. As an archival systems developer I have had the delight of seeing where the knowledge, skills, context, imagination and creativity of those who use my systems can take them. I've been challenged and inspired to innovate in order to support their needs, while at the same time embedding archival and recordkeeping principles into their practices. Standardisation does not have to be a straitjacket. If we get it right then it can be the building block for robust and resilient participatory archival networks, organic in nature, responsive to local community needs, but also connectable into broader global frameworks, and able to support multiple journeys through space and time.

Endnotes

1. David Bearman, 'Record-Keeping Systems', *Archivaria*, no. 36, Autumn 1993, pp. 16–37; Terry Cook, 'Electronic Records, Paper Minds: The Revolution in Information Management and Archives in the Post-Custodial and Post-Modernist Era', *Archives and Manuscripts*, vol. 22, no. 2, November 1994, pp. 300–29; Margaret Hedstrom, 'Descriptive Practices for Electronic Records: Deciding What is Essential and Imagining What is Possible', *Archivaria*, no. 36, Autumn 1993, pp. 53–63; Frank Upward, Sue McKemmish and Barbara Reed, 'Archivists and Changing Social and Information Spaces: A Continuum Approach to

Recordkeeping and Archiving in Online Cultures', *Archivaria*, no. 72, Fall 2011, pp. 197–237; Terry Cook, '"We Are What We Keep; We Keep What We Are": Archival Appraisal Past, Present and Future', *Journal of the Society of Archivists*, vol. 32, no. 2, 2011, pp. 173–89, doi:10.1080/00379816.2011.619688.

2. Anne J Gilliland and Sue McKemmish, 'Recordkeeping Metadata, the Archival Multiverse, and Societal Grand Challenges', in *Proceedings of the International Conference on Dublin Core and Metadata Applications 2012*, 2012, available at *<http://dcevents.dublincore.org/index.php/IntConf/dc-2012/paper/view/108>*, accessed 27 September 2012.
3. Andrew Flinn, 'Independent Community Archives and Community-Generated Content "Writing, Saving and Sharing Our Histories"', *Convergence: The International Journal of Research into New Media Technologies*, vol. 16, no 1, 1 February 2010, pp. 39–51, doi:10.1177/1354856509347707; Andrew Flinn, Mary Stevens and Elizabeth Shepherd, 'Whose Memories, Whose Archives? Independent Community Archives, Autonomy and the Mainstream', *Archival Science*, vol. 9, nos 1–2, October 2009, pp. 71–86, doi:10.1007/s10502-009-9105-2; Alexandra Eveleigh, 'Welcoming the World: An Exploration of Participatory Archives', presented at the ICA Congress 2012, Brisbane, 2012, available at *<http://www.ica2012.com/files/pdf/Full%20papers%20upload/ica12Final00128.pdf>*, accessed 7 May 2013; Isto Huvila, 'Participatory Archive: Towards Decentralised Curation, Radical User Orientation, and Broader Contextualisation of Records Management', *Archival Science*, vol. 8, no. 1, March 2008, pp. 15–36, doi:10.1007/s10502-008-9071-0; Katie Shilton and Ramesh Srinivasan, 'Participatory Appraisal and Arrangement for Multicultural Archival Collections', *Archivaria*, no. 63, Spring 2007, pp. 87–101.
4. Sue McKemmish et al., 'Describing Records in Context in the Continuum: The Australian Recordkeeping Metadata Schema', *Archivaria*, no. 48, Fall 1999, pp. 3–43.
5. Chris Hurley, 'The Hunting of the Snark: Looking for Digital "Series"', 2011, available at *<http://www.descriptionguy.com/images/WEBSITE/hunting-of-the-snark-search-for-digital-series.pdf>*, accessed 25 January 2014.
6. Sue McKemmish, Adrian Cunningham and Dagmar Parer, 'Metadata Mania: Use of Metadata for Electronic Recordkeeping and Online Resource Discovery', in *Place, Interface and Cyberspace: Archives at the Edge, Proceedings of the 1998 Conference of the Australian Society of Archivists, Fremantle 6-8 August 1998*, Australian Society of Archivists, Canberra, 1998, available at *<http://www.infotech.monash.edu.au/research/groups/rcrg/publications/recordkeepingmetadata-sm01.html>*, accessed 2 September 2012.
7. Chris Hurley, 'The Making and Keeping of Records: (1) What Are Finding Aids For?', *Archives and Manuscripts*, vol. 26, no. 1, May 1998, pp. 58–77.
8. McKemmish et al., 'Describing Records in Context in the Continuum', p. 8.
9. Wendy Duff and Verne Harris, 'Stories and Names: Archival Description as Narrating Records and Constructing Meanings', *Archival Science*, vol. 2, nos 3–4, 2002, pp. 263–85, doi:10.1007/BF02435625.
10. Sue McKemmish, 'Are Records Ever Actual?', in *The Records Continuum: Ian Maclean and Australian Archives First Fifty Years*, Sue McKemmish and Michael Piggott (eds), Ancora Press, Clayton, 1994, pp. 187–203.
11. Gilliland and McKemmish.
12. Duff and Harris; Gilliland and McKemmish.
13. Heather MacNeil, 'Picking Our Text: Archival Description, Authenticity, and the Archivist as Editor', *American Archivist*, vol. 68, no. 2, 1 September 2005, p. 272.
14. ibid., p. 276.
15. Christian Bizer, Tom Heath and Tim Berners-Lee, 'Linked Data – The Story So Far', *International Journal on Semantic Web and Information Systems*, vol. 5, no. 3, 2009, pp. 1–22, doi:10.4018/jswis.2009081901.
16. Nigel Cross, *Designerly Ways of Knowing*, Springer London, London, 2006, available at *<http://link.springer.com/chapter/10.1007/1-84628-301-9_1>*, accessed 21 January 2013.
17. Joanne Evans and Nadav Rouche, 'Utilizing Systems Development Methods in Archival Systems Research: Building a Metadata Schema Registry', *Archival Science*, vol. 4, nos 3–4, December 2004, pp. 315–334, doi:10.1007/s10502-005-2598-4.
18. Toby Burrows, 'Identity Parade: Managing Contextual Personal Information for Archival Data', *Archives and Manuscripts*, vol. 36, no. 2, November 2008, pp. 88–104.

19. Kathy Charmaz, 'Premises, Principles, and Practices in Qualitative Research: Revisiting the Foundations', *Qualitative Health Research*, vol. 14, no. 7, 2004, pp. 976–93, doi:10.1177/1049732304266795.
20. Sarah Wall, 'An Autoethnography on Learning About Autoethnography', *International Journal of Qualitative Methods*, vol. 5, no. 2, 2006, pp. 146–60.
21. Andrew C Sparkes, 'Autoethnography and Narratives of Self: Reflections on Criteria in Action', *Sociology of Sport Journal*, vol. 17, no. 1, 2000, pp. 21–43.
22. Carolyn Ellis, Tony E Adams and Arthur P Bochner, 'Autoethnography: An Overview', *Forum Qualitative Sozialforschung/Forum: Qualitative Social Research*, vol. 12, no. 1, 24 November 2010, available at <*http://www.qualitative-research.net/index.php/fqs/article/view/1589*>, accessed 23 January 2014.
23. Ciaran Trace and Andrew Dillon, 'The Evolution of the Finding Aid in the United States: From Physical to Digital Document Genre', *Archival Science*, vol. 12, no. 4, December 2012, pp. 1–19, doi:10.1007/s10502-012-9190-5; MacNeil, 'Picking Our Text'; Heather MacNeil, 'What Finding Aids Do: Archival Description as Rhetorical Genre in Traditional and Web-Based Environments', *Archival Science*, vol. 12, no. 4, December 2012, pp. 485–500, doi:10.1007/s10502-012-9175-4.
24. Clark A Elliott, *Understanding Progress as Process: Documentation of the History of Post-War Science and Technology in the United States*, Society of American Archivists, Chicago, 1983.
25. Processing *in situ* was often preferred, given the potential access it afforded to contextual knowledge 'in living finding aids, the minds of record creators and users', Hurley, 'The Making and Keeping of Records', p. 60.
26. Frank Upward, 'Structuring the Records Continuum: Part One: Postcustodial Principles and Properties', *Archives and Manuscripts*, vol. 24, no. 2, November 1996, pp. 268–85.
27. Sue McKemmish, 'Placing Records Continuum Theory and Practice', *Archival Science*, vol. 1, no. 4, December 2001, pp. 333–59, doi:10.1007/BF02438901.
28. Australian Science Archives Project, 'ASAP Annual Report 1996', 23 January 1998, available at <*http://www.asap.unimelb.edu.au/pubs/reports/1996/ar96_3.htm*>, accessed 9 September 2012.
29. ibid.
30. Peter Scott, 'The Record Group Concept: A Case for Abandonment', *American Archivist*, vol. 29, no. 4, October 1966, pp. 493–504.
31. Chris Hurley, 'Description', *Chris Hurley's Stuff*, 2012, available at <*http://www.descriptionguy.com/description.html*>, accessed 28 November 2013.
32. Barbara Reed, 'The Australian Context Relationship (CRS or Series) System: An Appreciation', in *The Arrangement and Description of Archives Amid Administrative and Technological Change: Essays and Reflections By and About Peter J. Scott*, Adrian Cunningham (ed.), Australian Society of Archivists, 2010, pp. 346–73.
33. Joanne Evans, 'Structure of the ADS', in *Archives and Reform – Preparing for Tomorrow, Proceedings of the Australian Society of Archivists Conference, Adelaide, 25–26th July 1997*, 1997, available at <*http://www.asap.unimelb.edu.au/pubs/articles/asa97/ADSStructure.htm*>, accessed 9 September 2012.
34. ibid. 'The idea is that all records identified in the accessioning process are documented at the series and inventory level. We aim to document the total records environment. Not only do the inventory, series and provenance tables contain archival documentation of records of continuing or long term value, but they also document other records created and used by an organisation or individual related to the surviving records, building a picture of the total recordkeeping environment. Varying the inventory unit ensures that high value records can be documented to a more detailed level then those of lesser value or those scheduled for destruction. In this way the ADS facilitates the systematic documentation of all records and what is done with them.'
35. MacNeil, 'Picking Our Text'.
36. Evans, 'Structure of the ADS'.
37. ibid.
38. Shannon Faulkhead, Joanne Evans and Helen Morgan, 'Is Technology Enough? Developing Archival Information Systems in Community Environments', *ESARBICA Journal*, vol. 24, 2005, pp. 74–95, doi:10.4314/esarjo.v24i1.30997.

39. Daniel V Pitti, 'Encoded Archival Description', *D-Lib Magazine*, vol. 5, no. 11, November 1999, doi:10.1045/november99-pitti.
40. Joanne Evans, *REEA – Building an Encoded Archival Description (EAD) Generator for the HDMS*, Australian Science and Technology Heritage Centre, July 2000, available at <*http://www.austehc.unimelb.edu.au/HDMS/HDMSeadreport.pdf*>, accessed 28 November 2013.
41. An example of this is the use of the indexing functionality by the South Australia Museum Archives, see <*http://www.samuseum.sa.gov.au/collections/information-resources/archives-search*>, accessed 28 November 2013.
42. Gavan McCarthy, *Guide to the Archives of Science in Australia: Records of Individuals*, D W Thorpe, 1991.
43. Gavan McCarthy and Joanne Evans, 'Mapping the Socio-Technical Complexity of Australian Science: From Archival Authorities to Networks of Contextual Information', *Journal of Archival Organization*, vol. 5, nos 1–2, 2008, pp. 149–75, doi:10.1300/J201v05n01_08.
44. McCarthy.
45. Tim Sherratt, 'Pathways to Memory', in *Proceedings of AusWeb96 – The Second Australian World Wide Web Conference*, Southern Cross University, 1996, available at <*http://discontents.com.au/words/articles/pathways-to-memory*>, accessed 14 September 2012.
46. Gavan J McCarthy and Joanne Evans, 'Principles for Archival Information Services in the Public Domain', *Archives and Manuscripts*, vol. 40, no. 1, March 2012, pp. 54–67, doi:10.1080/01576895.2012.670872.
47. ibid., p. 57.
48. For example ISAD(G), ISAAR(CPF), CIDOC CRM, Dublin Core, FRBR, EAD and EAC-CPF.
49. One of those bones that I know is buried in the OHRM artefact.
50. Tim O'Reilly, 'What is Web 2.0?', *O'Relly Media*, 30 September 2005, available at <*http://oreilly.com/web2/archive/what-is-web-20.html*>, accessed 15 September 2012.
51. Nikki Henningham, Joanne Evans and Helen Morgan, 'Out of the Shadows: Using Technology to Illuminate Women's Archives', in *Women's Memory: The Problem of Sources, 20th Anniversary Symposium of the Women's Library and Information Centre Foundation 17–19 April 2009, Kadir Has University, Istanbul, Turkey*, Women's Library and Information Centre Foundation, Instanbul, 2009, pp. 389–99.
52. Donald A Schön, *The Reflective Practitioner: How Professionals Think in Action*, Basic Books, New York, 1984.

Keepers of Ghosts: old signs, new media and the age of archival flux

Lisa Cianci and Stefan Schutt

Lisa Cianci is a professional archivist, multidisciplinary artist and new media developer. She currently lectures in Creative Arts programs at the College of Arts, Victoria University and is a researcher for the Keepers of Ghosts project at the Centre for Cultural Diversity and Wellbeing, Victoria University. Lisa's archival work has included her PhD project where she built an experimental, online archival system to explore creative practice and preservation of creative content, projects at the Australian Science Archives Project, consultancy work at Melbourne Information Management, setting up an archival system for the Frances Burke Textile Resource Centre at RMIT University and various freelance consultancy projects.

Stefan Schutt is a researcher at the Centre for Cultural Diversity and Wellbeing, Victoria University. Stefan's research interests revolve around digital technologies, social life and identity. Since 2001 Stefan has run virtual world, digital mapping, games, mobile phone and web projects for VU. Stefan is the co-founder of The Lab, a technology club for young people with Asperger's Syndrome, and creator of the Lewis & Skinner online signwriting document archive. For his PhD, he built an online system for creating and sharing life stories.

The Keepers of Ghosts project began when 10,000 records from a former sign-painting company were rescued from a demolition site in Melbourne's west. Beginning with the creation of an online archive, the project has since developed into an experimental research program of community outreach involving sign writers, shopkeepers, local history aficionados and people interested in 'ghost signs', or the remains of painted advertising signs. Here we discuss the project's investigation of the use of digital media to informally document and share otherwise-forgotten aspects of urban memory, and the proposition that the interplay between digital and physical archival activities can be harnessed to involve and connect diverse groups with shared interests, both at local and global levels.

Around the world, many thousands of people are using cameras on mobile digital devices to document traces of their neighbourhood's past before these traces disappear. In this article we focus on one such practice: photographs and other documentation of painted advertising signs, or 'ghost signs', which cannot be physically archived or collected because they survive, tenuously, on walls, shopfronts and hoardings.

Once taken, ghost sign photographs are posted to image-sharing websites, online forums and other social media, where communities of interest proffer and discuss their own images as well as reposted 'official' material from collecting institutions. Such 'wild archives'[1] generated by 'everyday practices'[2] enable collective memory and local urban documentation practices to develop in ways beyond the current scope and resources of custodial archives, a process that has been aided by the increasing ubiquity and mobility of networked digital devices, and the increasing ease and affordability of data transfer.

Here, we see the embodiment of Malraux's prescient notion of 'museums without walls':[3] free and open spaces for presentation of content previously held privately or by archives, museums, libraries or galleries. Social media is used to re-present fragments and glimpses of social and cultural history in ways that resonate with those who remember this history, have a related personal interest or seek an interaction with the past through the content assembled and shared by a group. As Laura Millar states:

> records are also created and used as safeguards against fragile and unpredictable recollections. It is here that the consideration of memory slips from individual to collective remembering.[4]

The online systems deployed for these collective processes are many and varied, and are increasingly used in combination. They include media-sharing platforms such as Flickr, Facebook, Instagram, Twitter, YouTube, Vimeo and Pinterest; online mapping systems such as Google Maps and Historypin; journaling systems such as Wordpress blogs and Tumblr streams; and dedicated online archival software such as Omeka.[5] Use constantly evolves as systems change and new services are developed. Combining systems through automated 'feeds' is increasingly being used to proliferate content accessibility and reach. For example, UK-based ghost sign aficionado Sam Roberts' Flickr feed of images is interlinked with a Wordpress blog, a Tumblr stream, Facebook page and Twitter profile.[6]

About the Keepers of Ghosts project

The Keepers of Ghosts project deploys an exploratory case study methodology[7] to examine how amateur digital practices, archives, current interests in urban history and memory, and community events can intersect in constructive and innovative ways. Undertaking a case study allows us to investigate a particular phenomenon in depth, the outcomes of which are not known in advance.[8] We have deployed the theme of historical painted signage to create the conditions under study: an online archive of signwriting documents and a related community intervention. This, as well as the fact that we are ghost sign aficionados ourselves, positions us, the researchers, as active participants in the research. Data generated by the project is currently being analysed and includes:

- a review of field practices: ghost sign photography and sharing; other amateur-driven digital history practices; signwriting history practices; online surveys undertaken with ghost sign practitioners;
- exhibition: semi-structured interviews with attendees, café owner and mural painter; attendance figures; comments in exhibition guest book;
- archival website: unique page view and visitor figures; site engagement via comments and additions;
- the researchers' process of undertaking the creation of both the archival website and the exhibition, as documented in a personal weblog (http://findingtheradiobook.blogspot.com).

One of the aims of this research is to better understand the motivation behind people's interest in ghost signs and related aspects of urban history. Indicative results to date suggest that this interest stems from a variety of motivations: personal recollection of brands or locations, experience or interest in the craft of hand-painted sign writing as well as design and typography, a fondness for local history or a desire to better understand the provenance of the neighbourhood they inhabit.

A further motivation, perhaps connected with some of those above, is a desire to explore urban spaces. Although this interest has long been documented in the work of artists and theorists from Charles Baudelaire and Walter Benjamin to the Situationists and Michel De Certeau, it currently appears to be undergoing a popular resurgence.[9]

Project history

Indeed, it is this same interest in urban exploration that led to the discovery of a cache of signwriting documents spanning 1915–1958 by one of the authors. In February 2012, Stefan Schutt discovered a pile of abandoned documents at a demolition site in inner-western Melbourne. The pile contained records of a former signwriting company, Lewis & Skinner (Figures 1, 2 and 3).

The documents included job sheets, drawings, photographs, painted mock-ups, instructions to sign writers, invoices, and letters to and from clients. Over the following year, 10,000 documents were scanned and uploaded to an online archive[10] built using a customised version of the open source archival system Omeka. It was a thankless task for the two workers undertaking the scanning of these less-than-pristine papers.

A grant from a local foundation provided limited resources to undertake the technical development and refinement, and the scanning and uploading work. However this funding did not cover detailed checking and proofreading, nor the inclusion of detailed metadata beyond basic job and geolocation details (something that Omeka is designed to support). A project decision was made early to privilege comprehensiveness of uploaded content over comprehensiveness of metadata, with a view towards seeking additional support later to undertake finessing.

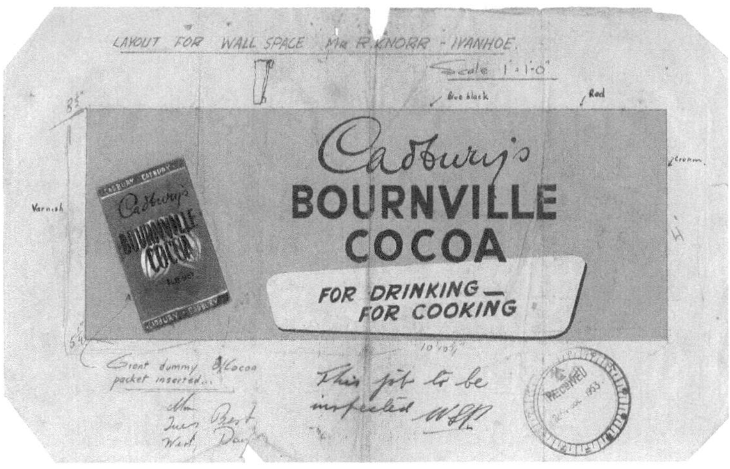

Figure 1. Layout for wall space, Ivanhoe, R Knorr, 9 February 1955, digitised document from the Lewis & Skinner archive (http://lewisandskinner.com/items/show/2596).

Figure 2. The 'find' records of Lewis & Skinner in situ at the Footscray demolition site, 2012, image by Stefan Schutt.

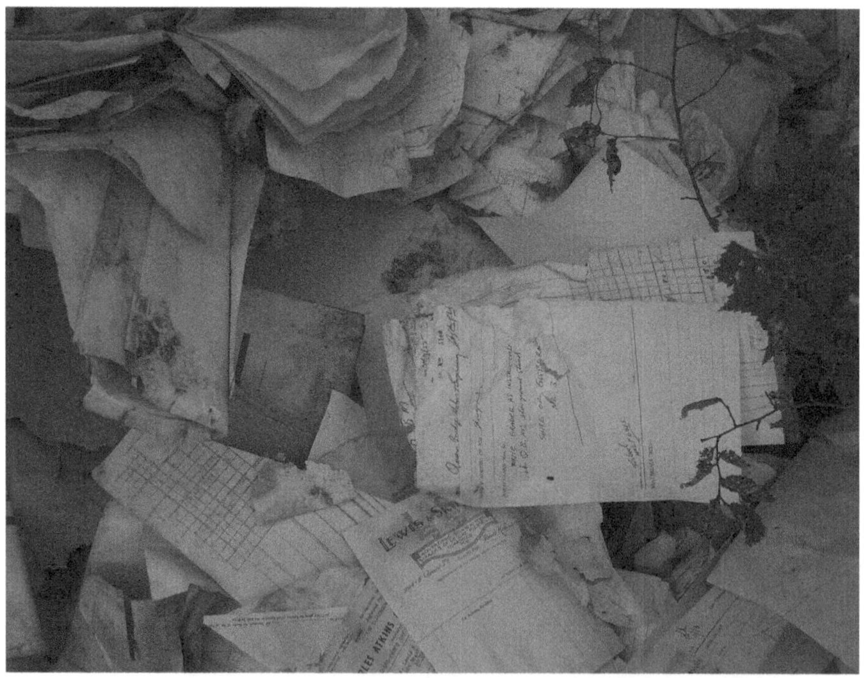

Figure 3. Detail of found records of Lewis & Skinner, 2012, image by Stefan Schutt.

For professional archivists, the incompleteness of Dublin Core metadata[11] may be problematic, but the choice was clear to the project team, and outlines one of the important issues involved in archival work: time and resourcing choices. In this case, project resources were geared towards providing as much basic and useful navigational information for the online public as possible. The records include descriptive titles with details of content and date, and the mapping provides location information. They are browsable and searchable via suburb, thematic tags and free text, but are a work in progress in terms of their accuracy, with occasional spelling and notation errors.

As the records were found dumped at a demolition site, we have no notion of original order or corporate knowledge of the organisation's history. Our research to date has only uncovered cursory location information about the Lewis & Skinner company. Although the sign painters interviewed as part of the subsequent exhibition program knew of the company, they were unable to shed any light on provenance information, although they have provided us with some leads.

The completion of the scanning and uploading of documents to the Lewis & Skinner archive was followed by a community outreach program. Designed to bridge the gap between the archive as a collection of inert documents and the living neighbourhoods represented in the archive, a community exhibition took place in October 2013 (see Figure 4), preceded by an academic seminar on ghost signs in March of the same year. A week-long exhibition of selected archive documents was held at a cafe close to where the documents were found.

During that week, a large Lewis & Skinner logo was progressively painted as a mural on the wall of the cafe by a local sign-painting artisan, with other sign painters joining in to help (Figure 5).

Figure 4. Partial view of the Lewis & Skinner exhibition in Seddon, 2013, image by Stefan Schutt.

Figure 5. Live sign painting of the Lewis & Skinner logo by sign writer and artisan Tony Mead and a volunteer sign painter at the exhibition in Seddon, 2013, images by Lisa Cianci.

The exhibition was preceded by the delivery of personalised postcards to residents at local premises represented in the archives, inviting them to share their stories about the sign, and to visit the exhibition (Figure 6).

The exhibition and sign-painting event created significant media coverage including television news reporting, radio interviews, newspaper and online articles, and was supported by the State Library of Victoria.[12] The project team counted 218 attendees through the week, although many more people visited during the evenings when the exhibition was also open, and the closing celebration which marked the completion of the logo sign painting.

Perhaps due to the diverse media coverage, a variety of different audiences was noted. A large contingent of current and former sign painters travelled from distant suburbs and regional Victoria to reconnect with their craft. Older visitors keen on local history also travelled long distances. Local residents attended, including families and local notables, as did young creatives attracted to the 'vintage' aesthetic of the graphic records. One local family had received an invitation in their shopfront letterbox, and came with stories of the 1950s Cadbury chocolate sign that had only recently been broken by vandals, and whose fragments they still kept. Another lived in a local building adorned with a ghost sign we had previously used to advertise a seminar (see Figure 7). The exhibition generated significant engagement and useful research information for us, plus a business and publicity boost for the cafe owner, who was himself a local with an interest in history.

A sign was painted on your building in 19 !

The find:
Last year, Dr Stefan Schutt from Victoria University stumbled on a pile of abandoned documents at a Footscray demolition site.

They were the records of Lewis & Skinner, a signwriting company that ran from the early 1900s to the 1960s. Stefan has now put all these documents on a website: www.lewisandskinner.com. They include details of signwriting jobs from all over Melbourne, for Mobil service stations, milk bars, shops and railway hoardings.

In those documents, Stefan found a job sheet that mentions Lewis & Skinner painting a sign on your building!

Here's the link: www.lewisandskinner.com//items/show/

The exhibition:
We would like to invite you to an exhibition of all the Lewis & Skinner documents from Footscray, Yarraville and Seddon. This is a community project run by Stefan and supported by Victoria University, the State Library of Victoria and Lady Moustache café.

As well as documents, there will be live sign writing every day of the exhibition from 12.00pm to 2.00pm, by local signwriting artisan Tony Mead. We also invite you to share the history of your building - either in the comments section of the website, or at the exhibition, where Stefan and team will be taking notes. Or you can contact Stefan directly, see details below.

For more information:
Call Stefan on 0410 387 622
or email him on: stefan.schutt@vu.edu.au

exhibition details
where: Lady Moustache café
84 Gamon Street, Yarraville
when: Wednesday October 2
to Sunday October 6
from 8am to 4pm
www.lewisandskinner.com

DOME 100

Figure 6. Template of personalised invitation given to residents of sites where Lewis & Skinner signs were located, 2013, produced by Lisa Cianci.

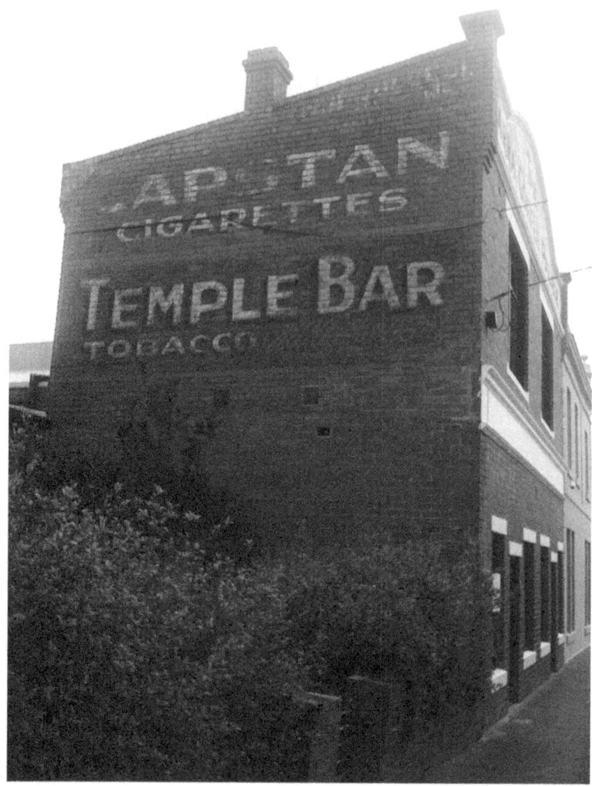

Figure 7. An example of a ghost sign – Capstan Cigarettes/Temple Bar Tobacco located in Yarraville, Melbourne, 2013, image by Stefan Schutt from his blog, available at http://findingtheradiobook.blogspot.com.au/2012/11/another-beauty-from-yarraville-plus.html, accessed 28 November 2013.

The nature of wild archives

Although social media systems are increasingly streamlined, the administration of online history groups nevertheless requires a great deal of volunteer-driven dedication and work.[13] This is perhaps why ghost sign assemblages tend to fall into a state of inactivity after some time. An example is the Melbourne-based ghost signs website 'Our Fading Past',[14] which is no longer actively maintained and has become a static digital archive itself. This raises the issue of who owns or controls these archives, and whether anyone will save or document these online archives in the wild?

User-driven social media – or perhaps more fittingly, *sociable media*[15] – also incorporate content from institutional collections. An example is the Facebook page 'Lost Melbourne',[16] which began in late 2012 and has since attracted a following of over 30,000. Lost Melbourne's followers post mostly digitised old photographs and film. Part of this content is sourced from institutional collections and sites such as 'Trove'[17] and part from followers' own collections. The content posted generates lively dialogues and even controversies.[18] Followers also use the page to request information from other followers about artefacts, places or people. Lost Melbourne has rapidly become a nodal point for collective memory about a city and its people. As Paul Ricoeur states: 'the archive is not just a physical or spatial place, it is also a social one'.[19] Through the medium of Facebook, which is predicated on online social interaction, the 'everyday practice' of repurposing archival content drives the creation of memory narratives from a variety of viewpoints. As we have seen in recent archival literature, archivists are seeking ways to utilise technology to 'open up archives as social "spaces of memory"'[20] – an emergent practice that amateurs have adopted, it seems, with gusto.

Ghost signs: mapping an international phenomenon

People have been interested in ghost signs for some time. Professional aficionados such as the US-based photographer and writer Wm. Stage[21] produced ghost sign books in the 1980s, coinciding with the decline of the sign-painting industry. In the 1990s, New York-based Frank Jump[22] became known for his documentation of the city's fading signs. Meanwhile, groups of current and former sign writers, such as the international organisation Letterheads,[23] have been active throughout in keeping the craft alive by running websites, forums and dedicated sign-painting weekends and conventions. Currently, the Sign Painter documentary and associated book[24] are generating significant worldwide interest.

During the consecutive development of the World Wide Web, social media and mobile technologies, interest in ghost signs exploded. One of the topic's many social media groups on Flickr[25] now has over 25,000 shared items posted by over 2000 members at the time of writing. Alongside this, recent years have seen a valorisation and resurgence of handmade craft of all kinds, as well as a concern for what has been called 'urban memory',[26] which is seen to be connected with a contemporary 'crisis of memory' in Western societies, 'a fear that the material traces of the past might be swept away, taking memory with them'.[27]

Academic interest in the ghost signs phenomenon is brewing. Through the Keepers of Ghosts project, we have formed links with a range of individuals and groups currently involved in the study of ghost signs and related digital archival practices and possibilities,[28] particularly 'the possibilities afforded by networked and digital technology … [to] … provide more spaces for public interaction for archives to directly contribute to memory production and propagation'[29] through tactics including crowdsourcing and dynamic online mapping.

A central question raised by such investigation is whether or not collections of ghost sign photographs (or, indeed, scans of ghost sign ephemera or other photographs of changing urban traces) could be considered archives. Here we refer to the three attributes of archives as defined by Verne Harris, Research and Archive Director at the Nelson Mandela Centre of Memory. These attributes are described as 'one, a trace on, or in, a surface; two, a surface with the quality of exteriority, and; three, an act of deeming such a trace to be worthy of protection, preservation and the other interventions which we call "archival"'.[30] Interestingly, Harris defines deeming in this context as 'almost without apparatus and certainly without professional or disciplinary authority. Anyone can deem.'[31] Under this definition, it would suggest that the answer to the question is yes. And although such collections may not conform to more traditional notions of the archive, they do demonstrate the multidisciplinary broadening of archival theory and practice – to 'enrich the discourse' – as recommended by Jacobsen, Punzalan and Hedstrom.[32]

But such a broadening is not without its problematics. Questions raised by our research include: how does the renewed interest in urban exploration and memory interact with concepts of the archive, including current discourse around the archive – memory nexus? For instance, does documenting physical sites count as evidence of their existence, or as the symbolic representation of collective memory? And how should we regard the transient nature of 're-presentation' of ghost signs? Imagine a digital photograph of an old sign. After it is taken, a copy is uploaded to a social media website. Here it is searchable by tags and surrounded by Global Positioning System (GPS) map references, comments and links to related content. What, then is 'core' content, and what is context and metadata? Who 'owns' which data, and for how long? Who maintains it? What happens when the 'variable media' system[33] on which it is stored changes or disappears? And is there ever a point at which a 'definitive' record can be deemed to exist, and if so, by whom?

Re-contextualising the archive: digital and physical activations

The physical Lewis & Skinner documents might be conceived as a finite, incomplete collection of records, but the digitisation project has opened up this collection as a 'living archive'[34] with all its potentials and ambiguities. It is now a collection that is continuously 'activated': edited and updated; exhibited; and re-visualised.[35] The meanings and understandings of the Lewis & Skinner documents have evolved with the ongoing generation of new contexts. GPS location data in the Omeka system has facilitated visits to former sign sites by users, leading to contemporary photographs of sites being added to the archive by way of the Omeka comment facility. As Tom Nesmith states, 'to the extent that an object (or record) can be known at all, it can only be known over time, as it goes through these processes of contextualization and re-contextualization, and more of its relationships with other records and actions are understood'.[36]

The accessibility of records in the Lewis & Skinner archive has also made it possible to develop Victoria University student projects, located in Melbourne's inner west. Thus far, two undergraduate groups (within the Bachelor of Arts and Diploma of Visual Art) have taken part via Omeka's 'exhibit' functionality. Interestingly, although the lack of surviving Lewis & Skinner signs proved disappointing to some students, most were still motivated by the project to research, visit and document other ghost signs. All agreed that their perception of local environments had changed, and in some ways, their everyday practices. Students commented on how they now look up at buildings as they walk through older urban areas, sometimes taking photos with smart cameras and 'blogging' their findings.

Such outcomes could not have been envisaged by the creators of the Lewis & Skinner records. For Eric Ketelaar, such activation of records assists the development of cultural identities: 'the meaning of a record or of any other cultural artifact must be understood in two different ways – first, the meaning *of* the record and second, the meaning *for* someone or *for* an occasion'.[37]

Other project activations involved the physical exhibition itself. This included creating a 1.2 x 2.4 metre map visualisation featuring 1945 aerial photographs of Melbourne's west overlaid with sign-painting job documents from the Lewis & Skinner archives. Lines pointed to the locations where the signs were painted (see Figure 8). Another activation was the live painting of the Lewis & Skinner mural, which took place for two hours daily during the exhibition week, and was inspired by other sign-painting 'performances' in the US. These activations were very different in form, but

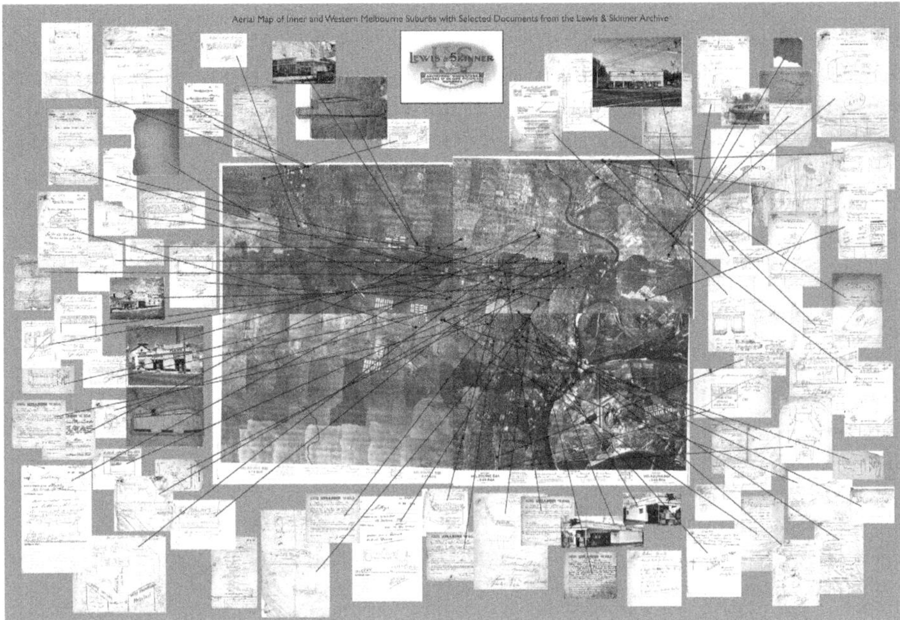

Figure 8. The 'Big Map' – visualisation of Lewis & Skinner records mapped to old aerial maps of Melbourne's west, 2013, visualisation produced by Lisa Cianci.

each generated engagement with the archives in particular, with the craft of signwriting, and local urban history in general.

Archives in flux

We have observed several issues relating to online documentation of ghost signs: some sites fall into disuse; online images are not always well documented with accurate and specific location or date capture; those documenting old signs don't necessarily use standard archival descriptors or the metadata may not be accurate; and there is no way to determine data veracity or authenticity other than community self-moderation via comments, tags and other inbuilt system functions.

Our research has raised a range of related questions for further investigation. What kinds of community-based strategies might we deploy to keep separate silos of thematically related content connected, relevant, authentic and accessible? Is there a role for collecting institutions and professional archivists and curators as stakeholders in wild archives? Or conversely (as we are now observing), should institutions aim to make their holdings available to the public in new yet controlled ways, thereby 'taming' wild archival practices? Can partnerships that involve jointly accessed data, such as the Powerhouse Museum's agreement with Historypin,[38] address the thorny issues of legacy, provenance and openness?

Further potential for investigation can be found in possible interactions between physical environments, layers of place-based digital presentation and crowdsourcing of content. Not much, for instance, has been written about combining mixed reality[39] with archives. Heritage projects utilising augmented reality[40] (AR) and GPS are emerging, such as the National Trust Victoria's 'Lost 100' iPhone app. This app 'superimposes images of demolished buildings over what is at the location now, by augmenting the iPhone's existing camera function': past meets present through the window of a smartphone screen.[41] Users can further augment this content by adding their own images and stories via linked Facebook and Twitter platforms. The Museum of London's 'StreetMuseum: Londinium',[42] as well as the GPS- and app-driven Indigenous tour of the Murray – Darling basin 'Ringbalin: River Stories',[43] provide further examples of the meshing of place, history and culture via digital content and AR technologies.

Our experimental activities using the Lewis & Skinner records have revealed the potential of hybrid methods of presentation, re-presentation and re-contextualisation – yet we have only scratched the surface of possibilities inherent in such different worlds colliding and collaborating. As Millar tells us, 'technology does blur the lines between "here" and "there" and "then" and "now"'.[44] However, Keepers of Ghosts is not only about past and present. It is also about future potential: reinvention, renewal and the recursive process of archive and memory interacting, and producing hybrid practices. But like any bright future promised by technology, we also need to keep a careful eye on the things that may be lost in the process, and take appropriate archival safeguards. The famous statement by the recently departed prophet of modernity, Marshall Berman, still applies today:

> To be modern is to find ourselves in an environment that promises us adventure, power, joy, growth, transformation of ourselves and the world – and, at the same time, that threatens to destroy everything we have, everything we know, everything we are.[45]

Acknowledgements

The authors would like to thank the Telematics Trust, Victoria University, the State Library of Victoria, Lady Moustache cafe, artist Carey Potter and sign writer and artisan Tony Mead for their assistance in realising the Keepers of Ghosts project.

Endnotes

1. 'Wild archives' refers to the term 'archives in the wild' used in Jeremy Leighton John with Ian Rowlands, Peter Williams and Katrina Dean, 'Digital Lives. Personal Digital Archives for the 21st Century >> An Initial Synthesis', Digital Lives Research Paper, 22 February 2010, Version 0.2, UK, p. vii, available at *<http://britishlibrary.typepad.co.uk/files/digital-lives-synthesis02-1.pdf>*, accessed 28 November 2013.
2. 'Everyday practices' refers to theories about everyday life (Anthony Giddens), mass culture and routine practices (Michel de Certeau). Michel de Certeau, *The Practice of Everyday Life*, trans. Steven Rendall, University of California Press, Berkeley, 1984. Anthony Giddens, *Modernity and Self-Identity: Self and Society in the Late Modern Age*, Stanford University Press, Stanford, CA, 1991.
3. André Malraux, *The Voices of Silence*, Princeton University Press, Princeton, NJ, 1953.
4. Laura Millar, 'Touchstones: Considering the Relationship Between Memory and Archives', *Archivaria*, no. 61, Spring 2006, pp. 105–26, p. 115.
5. The systems listed can be found at the following URLs (all accessed 28 November 2013): Flickr, *Flickr*, available at *<http://www.flickr.com>*; Facebook, *Facebook*, available at *<https://www.facebook.com>*; Instagram, *Instagram*, available at *<http://instagram.com>*; Twitter, *Twitter*, available at *<https://twitter.com>*; YouTube, *YouTube*, available at *<http://www.youtube.com>*; Vimeo, *Vimeo*, available at *<https://vimeo.com>*; Pinterest, *Pinterest*, available at *<https://www.pinterest.com>*; Google, *Google Maps*, available at *<https://maps.google.com.au>*; Historypin, *Historypin*, available at *<http://www.historypin.com>*; Wordpress, *Wordpress*, available at *<http://wordpress.com>*; Tumblr, *Tumblr*, available at

<*https://www.tumblr.com*>; Roy Rosenzweig Center for History and New Media at George Mason University, *Omeka*, available at <*http://omeka.org.*>.

6. Sam Roberts is a ghost sign hunter and aficionado, and the creator of the research and publishing initiative *Ghostsigns*, UK, available at <*http://www.ghostsigns.co.uk*>, accessed 28 November 2013.
7. Albert J Mills, Gabrielle Durepos and Elden Wiebe, *Encyclopedia of Case Study Research*, SAGE Publications, Thousand Oaks, CA, 2010.
8. Robert E Stake, *The Art of Case Study Research*, Sage Publications, Thousand Oaks, CA, 1995.
9. Bradley L Garrett, *Explore Everything: Place-Hacking the City*, Verso Books, Brooklyn, NY, USA, 2013; Moses Gates, *Hidden Cities: Travels to the Secret Corners of the World's Great Metropolises; A Memoir of Urban Exploration*, Tarcher, New York, NY, USA, 2013.
10. Stefan Schutt, 'Lewis & Skinner Archive', available at <*http://www.lewisandskinner.com*>, accessed 28 November 2013.
11. Dublin Core Metadata forms the underlying structure of the Omeka system used for documenting the Lewis & Skinner archives. Dublin Core Metadata Initiative, 'Dublin Core Metadata Initiative Wiki', 2012, available at <*http://wiki.dublincore.org/index.php/Main_Page*>, accessed 28 November 2013.
12. Media coverage included a Channel Ten News item, radio interviews on ABC Radio and many articles such as the following one in *The Age* newspaper that attracted a great deal of attention for the physical exhibition: Anabel Ross, 'Faded Signs Haunt Melbourne Streets', *The Age*, 28 September 2013, available at *http://www.theage.com.au/entertainment/faded-signs-haunt-melbourne-streets-20130927-2ujel.html*, accessed 28 November 2013.
13. The 'Lost Melbourne' Facebook page had a recent call for volunteers to assist with the administration of the page due to the high number of posts and comments which need to be moderated and extensive content that required management. Lost Melbourne, 'Lost Melbourne', 2012, available at <*https://www.facebook.com/LostMelbourne*>, accessed 28 November 2013.
14. Anthony Malloy, 'Our Fading Past', available at <*http://www.ourfadingpast.com/*>, accessed 28 November 2013.
15. Judith Donath, 'Sociable Media', *The Encyclopedia of Human–Computer Interaction*, 2004, available at <*http://smg.media.mit.edu/papers/Donath/SociableMedia.encyclopedia.pdf*>, accessed 28 November 2013.
16. 'Lost Melbourne'.
17. National Library of Australia, 'Trove', available at <*http://trove.nla.gov.au/*>, accessed 28 November 2013.
18. The authors and a third researcher, Prof. Marsha Berry, have co-written a paper on the 'Lost Melbourne' Facebook page: S Schutt, M Berry and L Cianci, 'Lost Melbourne: A Digital Ethnography of a Facebook Local History Group', *Global Ethnographic*, 2013, under review, available at <*http://www.globalethnographic.com/*>, accessed 28 November 2013.
19. Paul Ricoeur, *Memory, History Forgetting*, trans. Kathleen Blamey and David Pellauer, University of Chicago Press, Chicago, 2006, p. 167.
20. Trond Jacobsen, Ricardo L Punzalan and Margaret L Hedstrom, 'Invoking "Collective Memory": Mapping the Emergence of a Concept in Archival Science', *Archival Science*, vol. 13, nos 2–3, June 2013, pp. 217–51, p. 222.
21. Wm. Stage, *Ghost Signs: Brick Wall Signs in America*, ST Publications, Cincinnati, OH, 1989.
22. Frank Jump, *Fading Ads of New York City*, History Press, London, 2011.
23. Letterheads, 'The Letterhead Website', 2009, available at <*http://www.letterville.com*>, accessed 28 November 2013.
24. Faythe Levine and Sam Macon (directors), *Sign Painters*, film, USA, 2013. Faythe Levine, Sam Macon and Ed Ruscha, *Sign Painters*, Princeton Architectural Press, Princeton, NJ, 2012. Project information available at <*http://signpaintermovie.blogspot.com/*>, accessed 28 November 2013.
25. Flickr Group, 'Ghost Signs', available at <*http://www.flickr.com/groups/10285999@N00/pool/*>, accessed 28 November 2013.
26. Mark Crinson, *Urban Memory: History and Amnesia in the Modern City*, Routledge, Oxford, 2005.

27. ibid., p. ix.
28. This includes the aforementioned Sam Roberts (UK), Melbourne-based typographer and academic Stephen Banham, author of the book *Characters: Cultural Stories Revealed Through Typography* (Stephen Banham, *Characters: Cultural Stories Revealed Through Typography*, Thames & Hudson Australia, Port Melbourne, 2011) and Dr Laura Carletti from the Art Maps project at the Tate Gallery, UK.
29. Jacobsen, Punzalan and Hedstrom, p. 225.
30. Verne Harris, 'Genres of the Trace: Memory, Archives and Trouble', *Archives and Manuscripts*, vol. 40, no. 3, 2012, pp. 147–57, p. 150.
31. ibid.
32. Jacobsen, Punzalan and Hedstrom, p. 243.
33. The term 'variable media' is one used by the digital preservation community to describe analogue and digital media that exist in ephemeral formats. 'The Variable Media Network proposes an unconventional preservation strategy based on identifying ways that creative works might outlast their original medium.' Variable Media Network, available at <*http://www.variablemedia.net/e/index.html*>, accessed 28 November 2013.
34. Adrian Miles, '12 Statements for Archival Flatness', in *Performing Digital: Multiple Perspectives on a Living Archive*, David Carlin and Laurene Vaughan (eds), Ashgate, Farnham, forthcoming 2014.
35. Eric Ketelaar, 'Cultivating Archives: Meanings and Identities', *Archival Science*, vol. 12, no. 1, 2012, pp. 19–33.
36. Tom Nesmith, 'Seeing Archives: Postmodernism and the Changing Intellectual Place of Archives', *The American Archivist*, vol. 65, no. 1, 2002, pp. 24–41, p. 36.
37. (original emphasis), Ketelaar, p. 23.
38. We Are What We Do, 'Historypin', available at <*http://www.historypin.com*>, accessed 28 November 2013; The Powerhouse Museum Historypin channel, available at <*http://www.powerhousemuseum.com/historypin/*>, accessed 28 November 2013.
39. The term 'mixed reality' encompasses the 'virtuality continuum' from the 'real world' to the completely virtual, immersive environment. Paul Milgram, 'A Taxonomy of Mixed Reality Visual Displays', *IEICE Transactions on Information Systems*, vol. E77-D, no. 12, December 1994, available at <*http://www.eecs.ucf.edu/~cwingrav/teaching/ids6713_sprg2010/assets/Milgram_IEICE_1994.pdf*>, accessed 28 November 2013.
40. The term 'augmented reality' describes the imposition of a computer-generated image onto one's perception of the 'real world' thus creating a hybrid experience.
41. National Trust Victoria, 'Melbourne's Lost 100 iPhone app', Australia, 2013, available at <*http://www.nationaltrust.org.au/vic/national-trust-victorias-lost-melbournes-lost-100-iphone-app*>, accessed 28 November 2013.
42. Thumbspark Limited, 'StreetMuseum: Londinium', UK, 2012, available at <*https://itunes.apple.com/gb/app/streetmuseum-londinium/id449426452*>, accessed 28 November 2013.
43. Ringbalin River Stories Project, 'Ringbalin: River Stories', Australia, available at <http://www.ringbalin-riverstories.com/>, accessed 28 November 2013.
44. Millar, p. 108.
45. Marshall Berman, *All That is Solid Melts Into Air: The Experience of Modernity*, Penguin Books, New York, 1982, p. 15.

Convergence, connectivity, ephemeral and performed: new characteristics of digital photographs

Jessica Bushey

Jessica Bushey is a PhD candidate in archival studies at the University of British Columbia, Canada. Her research explores the trustworthiness of digital photographs in social networking platforms. She is a Systems Analyst and AtoM Product Manager for Artefactual Systems, the lead developer for ICA-AtoM open-source archival description and access software. She is an Adjunct Professor at the iSchool@UBC and teaches courses on non-textual records, online archives, and photographic records. From 2006 - 2010 she led the digitization project at the Museum of Anthropology, UBC in which 35,000 ethnographic objects were photographed and made available online http://collection-online.moa.ubc.ca/.

The recent convergence of digital cameras into mobile phones with Internet connectivity has provided the opportunity for individuals and organisations to adopt new image-making practices. The widespread use of photo-sharing and social networking platforms for sharing, accessing and storing digital photographs is presenting scholars in the social sciences with new areas of research that address the nature of digital photography. By examining the technological, social and cultural factors involved in contemporary image-making practices, scholars are presenting new concepts regarding the characteristics of digital photographs that impact archival activities aimed at managing and preserving trustworthy digital records. This article identifies and discusses the key concepts emerging from social science research on digital photography that are most relevant to the archival field. Analysis of the findings of these studies suggests that new technologies and social practices are changing how people use digital photographs and their expectations of permanence. Therefore, archivists need to be engaged in interdisciplinary discussions regarding the evolution of photographic practices and emerging characteristics of digital photographs in order to anticipate the management and preservation activities required to protect contemporary visual records for future use.

> … digital photography is revealed as a continuation of the user's practices enacted with the analogue medium; only it is faster, even less permanent and even more excessive.[1]

I. Introduction

With a combined daily upload of 800 million digital photographs to the most popular photo-sharing and social networking sites, Facebook (<*http://www.facebook.com*>), Instagram (<*http://www.instagram.com*>) and Flickr (<*http://www.flickr.com*>), the prolific use of the online environment for accessing and storing digital photographs is a growing area of research for social science scholars interested in visual communication and cultural and media studies.[2] The aim of this article is to introduce the topic of digital photographs created with mobile devices (for example, camera phone) and shared through social networking platforms to the archival community, with the intention of identifying new concepts being introduced by social science scholars that highlight the interplay of the social and the technical in the production and use of digital photography. In doing so, the article raises awareness within the archival community to potential issues that archivists may need to address in the near future when determining the value of digital photograph collections held in online environments. Exploratory in nature, the article presents the author's preliminary investigations into the trustworthiness of digital photographs in social networking platforms and introduces an interdisciplinary approach to the research topic. The article is organised into the following sections: I. Introduction, II. Concepts and III. Summary. The second section on concepts is further divided into the following subsections: i. Media Convergence, ii. Connectivity, iii. Ephemeral and iv. Performed.

In 1827, Joseph Nicéphone Niépce wrote to the Royal Photographic Society about the result of his extensive research 'on the manner of fixing the image of objects by the action of light, and of reproducing them by printing, with the aid of the known processes of engraving'.[3] To support his claim and encourage the Royal Photographic Society to fund his work, Niépce presented the first permanent photograph, an image of the view from the upstairs window at his French estate, Le Gras. He referred to his process for fixing light as 'héliographie' (Greek: helios, meaning 'sun' and graphein, meaning 'write'). Unfortunately, the Royal Photographic Society was not interested and Niépce entered into an agreement with Louis Daguerre, a Parisian diorama painter, in an effort to commercialise the process of 'fixing the image of objects'.[4] The following 180 years reveal a succession of photographic processes, techniques and equipment under the moniker of photography. Archival literature on the technology of photography examines the combination of processes, techniques and equipment used in the production of photographs, providing archivists and conservators with the knowledge required to support accurate identification of photographs and appropriate preservation activities.[5]

Contemporary research on digital photography by social science scholars approaches the expansion and proliferation of photography as an outcome of broader technological changes, such as mass production and global networks. The research is framed by social and cultural theories of late capitalism, materialism and consumption, and asserts that technological change is itself shaped by the social circumstances within which it takes place.[6] A number of these studies reveal that early reactions in the 1990s to the advent of digital photography, which heralded the death of analogue photography and the beginning of the post-photographic era, are no longer relevant.[7] Instead, what has surfaced is a recognition that some of the cultural conventions of traditional photography remain intact and shape the reception and use of digital image-making technologies, whereas other aspects have been completely transformed and introduce new modes of creating photographs which rely on interactions between software, file formats and protocols for information exchange that contribute to the meaning and use of photographs.[8] As individuals and organisations utilise online platforms for sharing and storing their digital photograph collections, it is important for the archival community to understand the interplay between technology and social and cultural factors in determining the content and context of contemporary photographs. Furthermore, the role of photo-sharing and social networking platforms as repositories for visual culture and social memory should be examined from the archival perspective in which consideration of ownership, copyright and privacy must be weighed along with ongoing accessibility and long-term preservation.[9]

A review of the social science literature on digital photography reveals a number of studies that focus on personal image-making practices that utilise mobile devices with built-in cameras, such as camera phones, tablets and laptops. The practice of personal photography as 'that which is done by non-professionals for themselves and their friends and intimates'[10] is unlike professional pursuits of photojournalism, law enforcement and fine art, in which issues of authenticity, reliability, accuracy and the truth-value of a photograph are prioritised.[11] In fact, manipulations of personal digital photographs are treated as 'deliberate acts of self-deception',[12] as opposed to acts that alter or destroy the photograph's trustworthiness. Historically, personal photography as a social practice developed in the late nineteenth century, following in the wake of institutional and commercial applications of photography.[13] The personal photograph was used predominantly as an aid to memory – images of loved ones and family members were represented and treated as keepsakes. The presentation of personal photography typically involved framing photographs and hanging them in the home, or gathering collections of photographs and mounting them to pages in a bound album. Personal photographs were rarely viewed outside of the home and were considered to be private, precious objects.

The growth of the photographic industry in the twentieth century provided services and cameras aimed at supporting the amateur photographer, and by 1970, the majority of American and European households owned at least one camera.[14] The popularity of photography as a personal practice is captured best by Susan Sontag in *On Photography*, '[r]ecently, photography has become almost as widely practiced an amusement as sex and dancing'.[15] In her seminal text, Sontag draws attention to the fragmentary quality of photographs; how easily they can be unmoored from their original context with the passage of time, and how quickly their new associations and groupings can present new readings.[16] Throughout the mid to late twentieth century a number of theories were advanced regarding the nature of photography and the construction of photographic meaning, including Allan Sekula's assertion that photographic meaning is determined by use, and John Tagg's claim that photographic meaning is found in the technical, cultural and historical processes in which photographs are used.[17]

Cultural theorists Rubinstein and Sluis make the observation that the initial adoption of digital photography by amateur photographers was limited by a number of factors including the cost of digital cameras, the lack of convenient methods for sharing digital images, and the complexity and cost of publishing images on personal websites.[18] Furthermore, it was not until digital cameras became affordable, viewing technologies improved (in-camera and through external devices), image storage expanded and transmission across telecommunications networks became available and reliable that personal digital photography gained widespread use. Rubinstein and Sluis assert that: '[t]he disappearance of the camera inside the telephone bonded photography to the most importance device of personal communications that ever existed – the mobile phone'.[19]

Findings of studies conducted by Van House on the transition of image-making practices from traditional film-based to contemporary pixel-based technologies reveal that the digital environment and changes in social and cultural approaches to visual communication encourage spontaneous, opportunistic image-making and experimentation.[20] Digital technology and its associated practices have increased the volume of images available; and as a result, people are accessing and using more digital photographs, including those made by family, friends and strangers.[21] Additional studies reveal how the use of personal photography has shifted in the past 20 years from being a tool for memory, to a means of communication.[22] Instead of documenting major events and family history, personal photography has evolved into a form of identity formation and a tool to chronicle everyday experiences. This is evident in the proliferation of the 'selfie' – a style of personal portraiture typically created with a camera phone. Studies on American teenagers and camera use reveal a preference for photography as social communication.[23] '[I]ndividuals articulate their identity as social beings not only by taking and storing photographs to document their lives, but by participating in communal photographic exchanges that mark their identity as interactive producers and consumers of culture.'[24] The growing interest in studying personal digital photography is attributed to the fact that prior to the Internet, access to personal photography was limited. The emergence of photo-sharing and social networking sites has provided a platform for individuals to deliver their images to millions of viewers (and researchers). Nevertheless, Van House suggests that personal digital photography, as an area of study, is being under-represented in academic research and lacking in theory.[25]In contrast, the most recent issue of the Journal of the Association of Canadian Archives, *Archivaria* no. 76, is dedicated to perspectives on personal archives, and the previous issue included an article by Jordan Bass entitled 'A PIM Perspective: Leveraging Personal Information Management Research in the Archiving of Personal Digital Records'.[26]

II. Concepts

The social science literature that explores digital photography through an examination of its technological, social and cultural factors introduces a number of concepts that are new to the discourse of photography and relevant to subsequent discussions within the archival community regarding the many contexts of digital photography. Following an extensive review of the literature the following concepts have been selected for examination: *media convergence*, *connectivity*, *ephemeral* and *performed*. During the review it became apparent that authors use different terminology to express similar concepts. For example, the concept of connectivity is also referred to as mobility and liquidity. Considering the interdisciplinary nature of this area of investigation, there is a confluence of theory and methodologies, which results in similarities and differences in the application of concepts. Attempts have been made throughout the following sections to clarify terms and explain differences by highlighting the context in which they originate.

i. Media convergence

Convergence is a term that is used in the social sciences to describe the technological, industrial, cultural and social changes in the way that media circulates within our culture.[27] Media convergence is the process whereby new technologies are accommodated by existing media and communication industries and cultures.[28] It is used to described the adaptation, merging and transitioning that occurs when old and new technologies converge. In the context of digital photography, media convergence can be used to reference the flow of photographs between cameras, mobile phones, computers and the Internet. At one time, these devices and their technologies were distinct and self-contained, but now they are recombined into a new distribution mode that incorporates various platforms and access devices. As a result, the way that people use media changes. For example, a mobile phone is now a camera, a phone and a personal computer, which enables the user to transmit and receive data as audio, image and text. Media convergence can be seamlessly integrated into devices so that users are left unaware of the layers of distribution involved in accessing and delivering their digital photographs. This can present a situation in which management of personal digital content is hindered due to a lack of knowledge about the actual processes and services involved.

Media convergence can present challenges for archivists who may be tasked with acquiring the digital photographs of a prolific artist or public figure that has donated their personal archives.[29] Unlike the relationship between donors and archival repositories that is discussed in the recent Council on Library and Information Resources report *Born Digital: Guidance for Donors, Dealers, and Archival Repositories*,[30] which addresses the key issues and stages in acquiring and transferring born-digital materials held on physical media including external hard drives and personal computers, the relationship with donors who have their digital photograph collections stored on photo-sharing and social networking platforms may involve consideration of the rights of the service provider as a third party. Additionally, if different services are used, such as Flickr, Facebook and Twitter (*<http://www.twitter.com>*), the challenge to establish the context of creation for digital photographs becomes increasingly complex as the image files may be scattered throughout different devices, accounts and platforms. If the donor has passed away without recording the passwords for the accounts, then legal action would be required to gain access (requiring the donor agreement contract as proof of permission). Depending upon the amount of time that has passed since the accounts were in use, the service providers may have purged their systems, gone bankrupt or been purchased by another entity. A reflection of the growing importance of controlling access to online accounts and managing passwords in the event of accidental or unforeseen death is the rise of 'digital life management' services, which offer subscribers the ability to manage passwords, synchronise multiple devices and assign an heir.[31]

Media convergence affects the routine use of different devices and processes at each stage in the creation, management and storage of digital photographs. Scholarly research into personal information management of digital photographs has produced findings confirming that an abundance of digital photographs stored on mobile devices and in multiple online platforms presents a significant obstacle to managing collections over the long term.[32] Without management activities, creators may be unable to determine the long-term value of specific photographs or collections and by default, they adopt passive solutions to preservation activities such as accumulation. As a result, creators become increasingly reliant on photo-sharing and social networking applications to provide management tools and limitless storage for their digital photograph collections. For example, Flickr currently offers new members one terabyte of free storage, which has the potential to encourage individuals to accumulate massive volumes of digital photographs; however, there is no assurance that the photo-sharing service provider will maintain ongoing access to the digital content.[33] With the majority of commercial online services being provided by third-party cloud computing infrastructure and delivered through layers of providers (all with their own service-level agreements), the care and handling of digital photograph collections is placed in the hands of for-profit companies who manage data for an exponentially large number of users. It is yet to be determined if ongoing access and long-term preservation of digital photographs, guided by the principles of archival science, is a priority for the owners of photo-sharing and social networking platforms, or even a possibility.

Social networking platforms provide information about their users' interactions, either through their own analytics or through third-party application programming interfaces (APIs).[34] Embedded metadata in users' photographs are also mined by APIs. This information is extremely valuable to private and public entities who are willing to pay social media companies to collect and/or purchase it; therefore, one might assume that as long as there is commercial value in providing free accounts to social networking sites, the digital photographs of millions of users will be stored for the long term.[35] Yet, as users of the photo-sharing site Instagram learned in late 2012, the terms of services (ToS) can be changed by the provider without prior notice to the customer.[36] Essentially the change in the ToS granted Instagram the perpetual rights to all images uploaded to their site for commercial purposes. The public backlash that ensued put enough pressure on the photo-sharing service provider that it withdrew the clause; however, the incidence has raised concern among professional photography associations and legal scholars in regards to the fairness of ToS and future consequences of such agreements on control over members' digital content.[37]

The extent of ToS agreements required by photo-sharing and social networking platforms invites further analysis by the archival community to determine the roles and responsibilities of service providers and customers in regards to issues of content ownership, copyright, and ongoing access and long-term preservation of digital photograph collections. Any number of changes to the ToS, including the addition of a per-use membership fee, could alter the current situation and potentially prompt members to respond with legal action and/or remove their digital content from the photo-sharing and social networking platform. Removal of digital content from social networking sites is neither an easy nor a predictable process. A survey conducted by the International Press Telecommunications Council as part of the Embedded Metadata Manifesto project reveals that downloading digital photographs out of some social networking platforms results in the removal of embedded image metadata from the image file header that are necessary for identifying the name of the photographer, image copyright and the date the photograph was taken.[38]Thus, the simplicity presented by converging cameras into mobile devices with Internet connectivity and accessing and storing digital photograph collections via social networking platforms that rely on cloud computing infrastructure should be thoroughly investigated in an effort to understand the complex web of technological and legal relationships introduced by new image-making practices. Furthermore, the impact of shifting notions of ownership, copyright and control needs to be assessed by the archival community if digital photograph collections held within social networking platforms are to be considered for future reference or use as records of social memory and cultural history.

ii. Connectivity

Connectivity is defined as '1) the quality, state, or capability of being connected; 2) the ability to make and maintain a connection between two or more points in a telecommunications system, or computer system'.[39] In the context of digital photography, connectivity is also referred to as mobility and describes the characteristic of digital photographs to change, to be acted upon by individuals and systems, and to continually transform through multiple representations.[40] The following section discusses the connectivity of digital photographs within photo-sharing and social networking sites and the characteristic of connectivity in the online platform.

In the last decade, digital photography has taken the place of film-based photography for most personal uses (for example, travel, family portraiture and events). The emergence of online photo-sharing and management sites like Flickr are encouraging individuals and organisations (through Flickr Commons) to share and manage their digital photographs (born-digital and digitised). In doing so, photo-sharing sites perform as online social networks that are characterised by visual communication. The process of sharing photographs is facilitated through the online application's graphical user interface (GUI), which provides a tool for uploading digital content to the site, as well as rich site summary (RSS) feeds, email and third-party plug-ins for image management applications (for example, iPhoto and Lightroom).[41] The process of managing (that is, classifying and organising) digital photographs involves collaboration with other members of the photo-sharing platform. For example, Flickr members are encouraged to give their contacts (that is, other members) the permission to add comments, ratings and tags to their personal digital photographs, which become associated by the photo-sharing application as metadata about the digital photograph and are used by the application to discover, search and organise images within the collection and across collections in the system.[42] The collaboration can take different forms, but it is characterised by the breakdown of boundaries between the producers of content and the users of content. When users contribute metadata to a digital photograph, they are transformed from consumers to producers and are engaged in a process of *produsage* (that is, the collaborative and continuous building and extending of existing content in pursuit of further improvement).[43] In the context of photo-sharing communities and online image-making practices, members acting as *produsers* (that is, participants who are users as well as producers of information and knowledge) are involved in a process that does not aim to create a discrete and complete product.[44] Unlike a traditional photographic print, which is fixed as a discrete object, the digital photograph is always connected to a system or interface, which enables changes to occur. In this sense the networked photograph is always in the process of becoming.[45]

Connectivity can be explored by the archival community as a potential challenge to establishing authorship and determining the necessary components of the digital photograph as a record. Unlike traditional photographs, which may be under the control of a single photographer, or identified as being created by an individual or studio, the digital photograph that circulates in photo-sharing and social networking platforms may potentially be treated as the expression of many contributors, including the system in which it is held. If the context in which the digital photograph is intended to be received is the social networking platform, which includes comments, ratings and likes, then these components of the record are integral to its meaning. Additionally, the digital photograph can be included in any number of collections (that is, photostreams) that belong to different members. Ownership of the images is rarely required in order for members to access or use digital photographs within the photo-sharing platform; yet, access controls can be set by the owner when uploading digital photographs into the online environment. Findings of studies on personal photography and social networking sites confirm a shift in attitudes about ownership and use. Interviews conducted by Van House with members of Flickr reveal a sense of public ownership over all the images accessed through the photo-sharing site, as if the photographs were a public resource.[46] Digital technologies make it easier to associate and re-associate photographs with different photographers, places and times, thus creating new collections and sequences, but more importantly – new meanings. By using the same online interface for access and storage, the boundary between public and private, owned and open, and communication and preservation is blurred.

Connectivity is also discussed as a characteristic of social networking platforms and their underlying database structure. Studies that explore the Flickr platform (that is, interface, algorithm, database and APIs) suggest that Flickr does not simply enable connections between photographs, humans and technology, but actually constructs them through metadata, software code and protocols.[47] Throughout the social science literature the underlying network database is likened to a fluid repository of visual culture; yet, there is no mention of a trusted custodian.[48] The mobility of networked photographs is discussed by Van House as giving images 'a life of their own' and acting as non-human agents moving within the online system.[49] In the actual operation of an archival repository, access to records and their use are determined by a combination of legal agreements with donors, intellectual copyrights, statutes and privacy acts. Establishing and monitoring these restrictions are the responsibility of the archival institution. In contrast, photo-sharing and social networking platforms typically place the responsibility for clearing legal copyrights and gaining permission to upload digital photographs onto the user. As outlined in ToS and/or separate privacy policies, the provider of the service will respond to complaints made by individuals about specific digital content and, if deemed necessary, the content will be deleted from the photo-sharing and social networking platform.[50] The efficacy of this approach has yet to be assessed by the archival community. It is very likely that the majority of visual content held within member accounts in social networking platforms has not been cleared for public access and thus may be unsuitable for acquisition by an archival institution.

It should be noted that another aspect of the social networking environment is the collection of information about its members. Whereas an archival repository retains statistical data on researcher requests for records to assist with managing the archives (for example, information can contribute to setting digitisation priorities or identifying conservation treatments) and to provide justification of operating costs to private funders and public bodies, the network database uses system metadata to track users' interactions with the database and metadata linked to the digital photographs to provide responses to search algorithms. In respect to tracking users' interactions, the system can reveal behavioural patterns which in turn are used to steer users' behaviour by adjusting the interface.[51] In regards to search algorithms for tagged metadata, the system can provide information that was never meant to be public, but that is available as a result of automated connectivity signals between tags and visual content.[52] Thus, the connectivity of the network database is mediating the user experience and could provide tech-savvy entities with access to information about members of social networking platforms that may be protected under privacy legislation. It would be interesting to apply postmodern perspectives on the participatory role of the archivist in constructing the meaning of archives to the ideology of the digital platform.

iii. Ephemeral

Ephemeral is defined as 'lasting for a very short time'.[53] In the context of digital photography the quality of an image being ephemeral is closely linked to its use as visual communication and not as an object to be permanently preserved. Unlike film-based photographs that require a series of processes (for example, capture, film development, print production) to create the final image, the digital photograph can be captured, edited and disseminated almost instantaneously. The shift in photography, from a time-based activity to one of immediate gratification, is a reflection of technological innovation and changing cultural attitudes. As a result, the social uses of digital photography have expanded beyond album making and framed keepsakes to include real-time Twitter exchanges.[54] Increasingly, the value of a photograph has been transformed from an object of permanence to a fleeting expression that is meant to be consumed and immediately destroyed.

Van House discusses image-making practices with mobile phones and Flickr, and suggests that new technologies and social practices are changing the temporality of images, resulting in photography as a form of visual communication, but without any expectation of permanence.[55] Furthermore, the potential for digital photographs to be easily deleted, lost and/or corrupted may encourage the change in attitudes about image-based activities from being geared towards permanence to embracing immediacy and the short term.[56] An example of this shift can be seen in the 2011 release of Snapchat (<*http://www.snapchat.com*>), a unique photo-messaging application that enables users to take photos, add text and send the images to a controlled list of recipients – with a time limit on how long recipients can view the received images (up to 10 seconds).[57] Once the time limit is reached, the digital photographs are deleted from the receiver's mobile phone. As of 28 October 2012, users of the Snapchat application were sharing 20 million images a day.[58] Its appeal is that users can focus on communicating with digital photographs and not have the burden of managing or storing them, nor the concern that the digital photograph may be repurposed by the receiver. This application epitomises the new attitude towards photography, one that values communication over preservation. Traditionally, value is expressed by collecting and permanently preserving photographs; however, the philosophy of Snapchat is '[t]here is value in the ephemeral'.[59]

In the context of the archival community, value in the ephemeral prompts a discussion about the value in forgetting. Records managers and archivists are aware of the need for retention schedules for certain classes of records, balancing access to personal information and protection of privacy, and the challenges introduced by digitisation and online access to archival holdings.[60] The extended life of digital information on the Internet is a growing topic of concern, as exemplified in the proposed new legal framework for the protection of personal data in the European Union.[61] The policy has three components: the right to oblivion of the judicial past; the right to oblivion established by data protection legislation; and the right to oblivion of personal data having an expiration date in the context of social networks. Essentially, the policy grants users greater control over their personal information being held by a company or government agency.

Application of the 'right to be forgotten' in the context of digital photography could be that a user deletes their Facebook account and under the new law, Facebook would have to ensure that all personal information about that user and their digital photographs were permanently deleted from the company servers and any third-party cloud-based servers that store data for Facebook (for example, Amazon web services). This process may appear straightforward; however, the growing complexity of services, the ubiquity of data mining, and repurposing of both digital content and member account information held by photo-sharing and social networking platforms make it challenging for companies to completely delete an individual's activity and presence within a system. The importance of controlling personal online information and content is prompting responses by companies such as Facebook, Google and Apple to provide services that increase user control over sensitive information in digital format. For example, Facebook recently purchased an application (drop.io) that offers private file sharing with expiration date settings to delete files; Google provides a method to set dates to exclude webpages from being included in search results; and Apple's iCloud allows you to synchronise privacy settings across devices.[62] The implications of digital photographs containing expiration dates have yet to be discussed by the archival community, but there are a number of potential issues including archival repositories being unable to acquire digital photographs with known deletion dates, or unknowingly acquiring digital photographs with deletion dates. From the perspective of records management in an organisation, policies would need to be in place to ensure that employees did not apply deletion dates to records designated for retention and transfer to the archives.

iv. Performed

Roland Barthes, critical theorist and author of *Camera Lucida*, describes the relationship between the photographic image and the actual person or place it represents as 'this-has-been', which can be interpreted to mean that the image is a pictorial representation of someone or something that was once in front of the camera, but is now no longer there.[63] Current approaches to understanding the immediacy and presence that characterise digital photographic practice are exploring digital photography as a performed practice that represents 'this-is-happening'. The performed practice is expressed in relation to how digital photography is used and the rhetoric of representation. Mette Sandbye's research findings on web albums (that is, logical organisations of personal digital photographs on Flickr, Facebook and Picasa) reveal that the volume of digital photographs on photo-sharing sites, their sequencing and their subject matter are presented in a manner that reflects the structure of cinema and enables the viewer to experience the unfolding (that is, performance) and occurrence (that is, presence) of the photographic moment.[64] Unlike traditional still photographs in which only one image might be captured to represent an entire evening or a special celebration, digital photographs are continually being created throughout any and all events, no matter how banal the activity. The ubiquity of photography as a practice has saturated daily existence to such a degree that people have trouble believing an event has occurred without visual documentation.

The performance of photography is traditionally considered in relation to the staging of the event in front of the camera prior to image capture, and in relation to the 'show-and-tell' of presenting an album of family photographs to another person. Sandbye introduces the performance of digital photography in the context of articulating and transmitting a feeling of presence.[65] This is achieved through the immediacy of uploading digital photographs to online platforms so that others can view the digital photographs and respond with comments, or links to their own digital photographs that might be related or highlight a similar experience. Sandbye points to other studies on personal digital photography that discuss the mundane nature of digital image content and the similarity between the multitude of digital photographs documenting a single event.[66] Furthermore, studies on photo-sharing communities suggest that once the digital photograph becomes part of the online environment, its performative function changes every time the digital photograph is accessed.[67]

A study of moblogging, the specific practice of creating digital photographs with mobile phones and uploading the digital photographs to photo-sharing platforms, has been conducted by Karen Wagner and her findings are discussed in 'Moblogging, Remediation, and the New Vernacular'.[68] Initially, moblogging was distinct from other digital image-making practices that involved digital cameras and websites; but, due to the growing appeal of camera phone photography, many social networking platforms are now making it possible to upload images directly from mobile phones. Wagner describes the way moblog stories evolve as a result of the interaction between the blogger and commentators (that is, users that participate in the blog by responding with comments, which are typically in the form of digital photographs transmitted from their camera phones).[69] The exchange of visual content drives the conversation between the moblogging members. Unlike film-based photography that requires a lengthy process of capture, development and printing before viewing, the practice of moblogging is characterised by immediacy (for example, visual content is uploaded in-the-moment) and the experience of the image-based conversation can occur in real time.[70] The instant publication of mobile phone images compresses the traditional time between production and consumption of photographic images, likening the exchange to 'being-there'. Wagner observes that the immediacy of the relationship is expressed in moblogging habits, which include posting a digital photograph that presents specific visual content, such as a coffee cup in the morning or a bottle of beer at the end of the work day, that signal to other moblogging members who understand this type of image content as the moblogging vernacular for 'ready to communicate'.[71]

The concept of performed practice in the context of digital photography may not introduce additional challenges to archivists that have not already been addressed in earlier sections of this article; yet, it is worthwhile for the archival community to be aware of external disciplinary perspectives that explore new ways of understanding digital photography and its use. The concept of performed practice alters traditional notions of how photographs are used, the relationships drawn between photographs within an online collection and the environments in which exchanges and communications are taking place.

III. Summary

Personal digital photography has been made visible to the world through photo-sharing and social networking platforms. The traditional private practice of personal photography has become a public activity that is facilitated by media convergence and characterised by the qualities of connectivity, ephemeral and performed. Social science scholars exploring photography as a practice that is defined by social, cultural and technological forces are producing research that identifies the continuity of image-making practices and the ruptures in which digital practice departs from pictorial traditions. With an emphasis on practice, researchers are providing archivists with valuable information about the technologies and social activities that individuals are adopting to create, manage, use and store their digital photograph collections. The role of media convergence in shaping how individuals interact with photographic devices and online platforms cannot be understated. This article has focused on the characteristics of contemporary digital photographs; yet, it is important to be aware that media convergence invokes obsolescence as technologies rise and fall from use and social habits respond to new modes of visual communication. As the documentary universe evolves, archivists and information professionals will need to remain engaged and ready to explore the characteristics of records and changing practices of record-making and recordkeeping. The social science research on digital photographs and social networking platforms, and related discussions addressing the database as an archives, present an exciting opportunity for archivists, who are informed by archival theory and methodology, to engage and contribute their valuable perspective.

Due to the available literature, this article has focused on concepts related to digital image-making practices of individuals; thus, an exploration of digital photographs in organisational and institutional contexts would be useful to determine if the characteristics of connectivity, ephemeral and performed are inherent to all digital photographs in online environments. The cultural factor would be different, but as more organisations allow employees to use personal mobile devices to conduct business activities, the potential for similarities between individual and organisational digital image-making practices exists.[72] Furthermore, as organisations embrace cloud computing services for on-demand applications, platform interoperability and unlimited storage, the issues of data ownership, controlling access and storage of records that are subject to privacy laws, and managing content under copyright, will need to be addressed prior to signing ToS agreements with service providers. This is especially true for archival institutions that are considering adoption of cloud computing services for their digital repositories.[73] As stated in the introduction to this article, this is a preliminary investigation into digital photographs in social networking sites. Future research activities include a web-based survey questionnaire, in-depth interviews, and analysis of photo-sharing and social networking ToS agreements.

Endnotes

1. Joanna Zylinska, 'On Bad Archives, Unruly Snappers and Liquid Photographs', *Photographies*, vol. 3, no. 2, 2010, p. 147.
2. Cooper Smith, 'Snapchat Users Are Sending 400 Million "Snaps" Daily, Edging Past Facebook's Photo-Upload Volume', *Business Insider*, 19 November 2013, available at <*http://www.businessinsider.com/snapchat-edges-past-facebook-in-photos-2013-11*>, accessed 22 January 2014; Ian Brown, 'Humanity Takes Millions of Photos Every Day. Why Are Most So Forgettable?', *The Globe and Mail*, June 2013, available at <*http://www.theglobeandmail.com/life/humanity-takes-millions-of-photos-every-day-why-are-most-so-forgettable/article12754086/?page=all*>, accessed 29 December 2013.
3. Joseph N Niépce, *Notice sur l'Heliographie*, December 1827. Translation cited in The Harry Ranson Center, 'The First Photograph', University of Texas at Austin, available at <*http://www.hrc.utexas.edu/exhibitions/permanent/firstphotograph/history/#top*>, accessed 29 December 2013.
4. Graham Harrison, 'The History Men: Helmut Gernsheim and Nicéphore Niépce', Photo Histories: The Photographers' History of Photography Blog, 1 May 2013, available at <*http://www.photohistories.com/Photo-Histories/59/the-history-men-helmut-gernsheim-and-nicephore-niepce*>, accessed 29 December 2013.
5. Gerald J Munoff and Mary Lynn Ritzenthaler, 'History of Photographic Processes', in *Photographs: Archival Care and Management*, Mary Lynn Ritzenthaler and Diane Vogt-O'Connor (eds), Society of American Archivists, Chicago, 2008, pp. 22–58.
6. Judy Wajcman, 'Addressing Technological Change: The Challenge to Social Theory', *Current Sociology*, vol. 50, no. 3, May 2002, p. 351; Martin Hand, *Ubiquitous Photography*, Polity Press, Cambridge, 2012, p. 25.
7. Technology was acknowledged as an element in the transition from film to digital, but the discussions were limited to comparisons of the material object versus the virtual bitstream, and the loss of the original in the digital environment. Timothy Drucker (ed.), *Electronic Culture: Technology and Visual Representation*, Aperture, New York, 1996.
8. Martin Hand, p. 142; William J Mitchell, *The Reconfigured Eye: Visual Truth in the Post-photographic Era,* MIT Press, Cambridge, MA, 1992. For a discussion of digital photography as a socio-technical practice see Eric T Meyer, 'Socio-Technical Perspectives on Digital Photography in Professional Practice', PhD thesis, Indiana University, 2005.
9. Luc Pauwels, 'A Private Visual Practice Going Public? Social Functions and Sociological Research Opportunities of Web-Based Family Photography', *Visual Studies*, vol. 23, no. 1, April 2008, p. 35; Marita Sturken, 'Memory, Consumerism and Media: Reflections on the Emergence of the Field', *Memory Studies*, vol. 1, no. 1, 2008, pp. 73–8.
10. Nancy A Van House, 'Personal Photography, Digital Technologies and the Uses of the Visual', *Visual Studies*, vol. 26, no. 1, June 2011, p. 125.
11. Matt Carlson, 'THE REALITY OF A FAKE IMAGE, New Norms, Photojournalistic Craft, and Brian Walski's Fabricated Photograph', *Journalism Practice*, vol. 3, no. 2, 2009, pp. 125–39; Jill Witkowski, 'Can Juries Really Believe What they See? New Foundational

Requirements for the Authentication of Digital Images', *Washington University Journal of Law & Policy*, vol. 10, 2009, pp. 267–94.

12. Pauwels, p. 36.
13. Margery S Long and Mary Lynn Ritzenthaler, 'Photographs in Archival Collections', in Mary Lynn Ritzenthaler and Diane Vogt-O'Connor (eds), *Photographs: Archival Care and Management*, Society of American Archivists, Chicago, 2008, pp. 1–21.
14. José van Dijck, 'Flickr and the Culture of Connectivity: Sharing Views, Experiences, Memories', *Memory Studies*, vol. 4, no. 4, 2010, p. 60.
15. Susan Sontag, *On Photography*, Farrar, Straus & Giroux, New York, 1977, p. 8.
16. ibid.
17. Allan Sekula, 'On the Invention of Photographic Meaning', in *Thinking Photography*, Victor Burgin (ed.), pp. 84–109, MacMillan Press, London, 1982, p. 94; John Tagg, *The Burden of Representation*, University of Minnesota Press, Minneapolis, 1993, p. 118.
18. Daniel Rubinstein and Katrina Sluis, 'A Life More Photographic', *Photographies*, vol. 1, no. 1, 2008, p. 12.
19. ibid., p. 15.
20. The findings are drawn from a number of related studies, conducted from 2005 to 2011. The studies involved interviews of American photographers and photo elicitation (both analogue and digital sources). Van House, pp. 127–28.
21. ibid., p. 130.
22. van Dijck, p. 60.
23. Diane J Schiano, Coreena P Chen and Ellen Isaacs, 'How Teens Take, View, Share and Store Photos', *Proceedings of the Conference on Computer-Supported Co-operative Work*, New York, 2002. Cited in van Dijck, p. 61.
24. van Dijck, p. 63.
25. Van House, p. 125.
26. *Archivaria*, no. 76, Fall 2013, pp. 1–167; Jordan Bass, 'A PIM Perspective: Leveraging Personal Information Management Research in the Archiving of Personal Digital Records', *Archivaria*, no. 75, Spring 2013, pp. 5–48.
27. Henry Jenkins, *Convergence Culture: Where Old and New Media Collide*, New York University Press, New York, 2006. Cited in Tim Dwyer, *Media Convergence*, McGraw-Hill Professional Publishing, Maidenhead, 2010, p. 24; Nancy A Van House and Elizabeth Churchill, 'Technologies of Memory: Key Issues and Critical Perspectives', *Memory Studies*, vol. 1, no. 3, 2008, p. 304.
28. Dwyer, p. 2.
29. Archivists have published accounts of working with born-digital materials created by individuals (for example, Salman Rushdie); however, the digital content was contained on personal computers and external discs. Laura Carroll, Erika Farr, Peter Hornsby and Ben Ranker, 'A Comprehensive Approach to Born-Digital Archives', *Archivaria*, no. 72, Fall 2011, pp. 61–92.
30. Gabriela Redwine, Megan Barnard, Kate Donovan, Erika Farr, Michael Forstrom, Will Hansen, Jeremy Leighton John, Nancy Kuhl, Seth Shaw and Susan Thomas, *Born Digital: Guidance for Donors, Dealers, and Archival Repositories*, CLIR Report No. 159, Council on Library and Information Resources, Washington, DC, 2013.
31. Legacy Locker is a service that allows subscribers to manage their online accounts and passwords and assign an heir to inherit access to this information upon the event of their death. Legacy Locker was recently acquired by PasswordBox and is now offered as one of their services. See Legacy Locker, 'How Does it Work', PasswordBox website, 2013, available at <*https://www.passwordbox.com/legacylocker*>, accessed 29 December 2013.
32. Van House, p. 130.
33. Flickr.com is an online photo management and sharing application. Yahoo!, 'About Flickr', Flickr.com, available at <*http://www.flickr.com/about/*>, accessed 30 May 2013. Using the storage calculation tool provided on the Flickr website, one terabyte of storage is sufficient to store 218,453 digital photographs (@ 4.8MB). Flickr.com, available at <*http://www.flickr.com/#storage*>, accessed 12 November 2013.
34. Ryan Gallagher, 'Software That Tracks People on Social Media Created by Defence Firm', *The Guardian*, 10 February 2013, available at <*http://www.guardian.co.uk/world/2013/feb/10/software-tracks-social-media-defence*>, accessed 12 November 2013.

35. As a database, Flickr functions as a source of information on user interactions when accessed using specific APIs. Flickr allows researchers (academic and commercial) access to its metadata by granting API licenses so that they can create programs or services based on Flickr resources. José van Dijck, 'Flickr and the Culture of Connectivity: Sharing Views, Experiences, Memories', *Memory Studies*, vol. 4, no. 4, 2010, p. 401 and n. 2.
36. Matt Warman, 'Facebook's Instagram Claims "Perpetual" Rights to Users' Photos', *The Telegraph*, 18 December 2012, available at *<http://www.telegraph.co.uk/technology/social-media/9752288/Facebooks-Instagram-claims-perpetual-rights-to-users-photos.html>*, accessed 12 November 2013.
37. Ross Buntrock and Jason Madden, '#Know Your(Copy)Rights: Applying a Legal Filter to Instagram's Revised Terms of Use', in *The Instagram Papers,* ASMP, 2013, pp. 16–20, available at <http://asmp.org/pdfs/KnowYour(Copy)Rights.pdf>, accessed 22 January 2014.
38. David Riecks, 'Social Media Networks Stripping Data From Your Digital Photos', Library of Congress Blog, 11 April 2013, available at *<http://blogs.loc.gov/digitalpreservation/2013/04/social-media-networks-stripping-data-from-your-digital-photos/>*, accessed 12 November 2013; for a link to the results, see David Riecks, 'The Controlled Vocabulary Survey Regarding the Preservation of Photo Metadata by Social Media Websites', *Controlled Vocabulary Website*, 2009–2013, available at *<https://spreadsheets.google.com/pub?key=tceeIYNw8ZDC0N52UgRcgnA&single=true&gid=0&output=html>*, accessed 12 November 2013.
39. *Merriam-Webster Online*, s.v. 'connectivity', available at *<http://www.merriam-webster.com/dictionary/connectivity>*, accessed 30 May 2013.
40. Hand, p. 26.
41. Yahoo!, 'Getting Your Stuff Onto Flickr', available at *<http://www.flickr.com/tools/>*, accessed 12 November 2013.
42. Yahoo!, 'About Flickr', available at *<http://www.flickr.com/about/>*, accessed 12 November 2013.
43. Axel Bruns, 'Towards Produsage: Futures for User-Led Content Production', in *Proceedings Cultural Attitudes Towards Communication and Technology*, Fay Sudweeks, Herbert Hrachovec and Charles Ess (eds), Tartu, Estonia 2006, pp. 275–84, available at *<http://eprints.qut.edu.au/4863/1/4863_1.pdf>*, accessed 30 December 2013. Author-version of article consulted, Future for User-Led Content Production, QUT ePrints, pp.1-14. See also Produsage.org, 'Produsage: A Working Definition', 31 December 2007, available at *<http://produsage.org/produsage>*, accessed 12 November 2013.
44. Bruns, p. 2.
45. The process of becoming is an underlying philosophy of the Flickr company. See Flickr.-com, available at *<http://www.flickr.com/photos/josiahslove/3549028015/>*, accessed 12 November 2013.
46. Flickr supports Creative Commons licensing, which allows owners to specify the conditions for re-use; however, the notion of all images in the Flickr site as public resources is not accurate. Van House, p. 128.
47. van Dijck, p. 402.
48. Zylinska, p. 148.
49. Van House, p. 128. The idea that digital photographs become actors or non-human agents through their metadata and computer to computer communication is touched upon by Martin Hand and Michele Ashley Scarlett. Hand, p. 54; and Michele Ashley Scarlett, 'Remediating Photography: Re-Imagining Ethics In-Light of Online Photo-Sharing Practices', Master's thesis, Queen's University, Ontario, 2010, p. 51.
50. Flickr.com, 'Flickr Community Guidelines', available at <https://www.flickr.com/help/guidelines/>, accessed 12 November 2013; and Yahoo.com, 'Yahoo!Privacy Centre', available at *<http://info.yahoo.com/privacy/ca/yahoo/>*, accessed 12 November 2013.
51. van Dijck, p. 403.
52. K Lerman and L Jones, 'Social Browsing on Flickr', in *Proceedings of International Conference on Weblogs and Social Media* (ISCWM), 2007, available at *<arxiv.org/abs/cs/0612047v1/>*. Cited in van Dijck, p. 405.
53. *Oxford Dictionary Online*, s.v. 'ephemeral', available at *<http://oxforddictionaries.com/definition/english/ephemeral>*, accessed 2 June 2013.

54. Twitter includes the ability to add digital photographs to tweets, but the image metadata is removed. Twitter, 'Posting Photos on Twitter', last updated 2013, available at <*http://support.twitter.com/articles/20156423-posting-photos-on-twitter*>, accessed 30 December 2013.
55. Nancy A Van House, 'Personal Photos as Communicative Resources', unpublished manuscript. Cited in Van House and Churchill, pp. 295–310.
56. Van House, p. 130.
57. Snapchat, 'About', last updated 2013, available at <*http://www.snapchat.com/#*>, accessed 12 November 2013.
58. Snapchat, '1 Billion', Snapchat Blog, available at <*http://blog.snapchat.com/post/34536597612/1-billion*>, accessed 12 November 2013.
59. Snapchat, 'Philosophy', last updated 2013, available at <*http://www.snapchat.com/#*>, accessed 12 November 2013.
60. Eric Ketelaar, 'The Right to Know, the Right to Forget? Personal Information in Public Archives', *Archives and Manuscripts*, vol. 23, no. 1, 1995, pp. 8–17; Malcolm Todd, 'Power, Identity, Integrity, Authenticity, and the Archives: A Comparative Study of the Application of Archival Methodologies to Contemporary Privacy', *Archivaria*, no. 61, Spring 2006, pp. 181–214. For the impact of the Canadian *Personal Information Act* (Bill C-6) on archives, see Tim Cook, 'Archives and Privacy in a Wired World: The Impact of the *Personal Information Act* (Bill C-6) on Archives', *Archivaria*, no. 53, Spring 2002, pp. 94–115.
61. European Commission, 'Proposal for a Regulation of the European Parliament and of the Council on the Protection of Individuals With Regard to the Processing of Personal Data and on the Free Movement of Such Data (General Data Protection Regulation)', Explanatory Memorandum, 2012, available at <*http://ec.europa.eu/justice/data-protection/document/review2012/com_2012_11_en.pdf*>, accessed 30 December 2013; and Jeffrey Rosen, 'The Right to be Forgotten', *Stanford Law Review*, 13 February 2012, available at <*http://www.stanfordlawreview.org/online/privacy-paradox/right-to-be-forgotten*>, accessed 12 November 2013.
62. Stuart Jeffries, 'Why We Must Remember to Delete – and Forget – in the Digital Age', *The Guardian*, 30 June 2011, available at <*http://www.guardian.co.uk/technology/2011/jun/30/remember-delete-forget-digital-age*>, accessed 12 November 2013.
63. Roland Barthes, *Camera Lucida*, trans. Richard Howard, Farrar, Straus and Giroux, New York, 1980, p. 76. Cited in Mette Sandbye, 'It Has Not Been – it *is*. The Signaletic Transformation of Photography', *Journal of Aesthetics & Culture*, no. 4, 2012, p. 1.
64. Sandbye, p. 2.
65. ibid., p. 4.
66. Susan Murray, 'Digital Images, Photo-Sharing, and our Shifting Notions of Everyday Aesthetics', *Journal of Visual Culture*, vol. 7, 2008, pp. 147–63; Søren Mørk Petersen, 'Common Banality: The Affective Character of Photo Sharing, Everyday Life and Produsage Cultures', PhD dissertation, IT University of Copenhagen, 2008. Cited in Sandbye, p. 7.
67. van Dijck, p. 72.
68. The research project entitled 'From Celluloid to Pixels. Network and Ritual Around e-Cinema and Mobile Phone Camera' (2006–2008) was conducted by Karin Wagner with funding from the Swedish Research Council. The methodology included a number of online surveys and interviews. Karin Wagner, 'Moblogging, Remediation, and the New Vernacular', *Photographies*, vol. 4, no. 2, September 2011, pp. 224–25, n. 4 & 5.
69. ibid., p. 212.
70. The practice of polaroid photography contains attributes of immediacy and experience, but the dissemination of the polaroid prints requires receivers to be in physical contact with the photographer at the time of the image-taking event, or within postal range. In this manner, polaroid photography is limited by time and space – it is missing the critical component of digital photography, which is connectivity.
71. Wagner, p. 214.
72. Policies and procedures for digital photography creation and use would be required in an organisational or institutional setting. Cloud Security Alliance, 'Security Guidance for Critical Areas of Mobile Computing', v.1.0., Mobile Working Group, 2012, pp. 1–11.
73. Kirsten Ferguson-Boucher and Nicole Convery, 'Storing Information in the Cloud – A Research Project', *Journal of the Society of Archivists*, vol. 32, no. 2, 2011, pp. 221–39. doi: 10.1080/00379816.2011.619693.

Visualising Famagusta: interdisciplinary approaches to the study of the Orthodox Cathedral of Saint George of the Greeks in Famagusta, Cyprus

Sven J Norris, Michael JK Walsh and Thomas A Kaffenberger

Sven J Norris received his BA (Hons) in Interior Architecture at the University of Wales Institute, Cardiff in 2000 and completed his Masters in Computer Arts at Thames Valley University (University of West London) in 2002. He has worked as a freelancer, contractor and full-time employee in industry within the fields of new media, designing and developing screen-based media and content for companies and agencies including Arc Worldwide, Leo Burnett Group, Reuters, and McKinsey & Co. For the past six years, Sven has been a faculty member at Nanyang Technological University's School of Art, Design & Media in Singapore, where he teaches areas he is passionate about including screen-based media, and web and game design. His main interests revolve around the creation and evolution of real-time virtual environments in the areas of entertainment, education and more recently cultural heritage.

Michael Walsh is Associate Chair (Research) of the School of Art, Design and Media at Nanyang Technological University, Singapore. He has written several books on the artist CRW Nevinson, the first of which was *This Cult of Violence* (Yale University Press, 2002). He has also edited several books investigating the relationship between Modernism and the Great War, the most recent being *London, Modernism and 1914* (Cambridge University Press, 2010). In 2011 he published *Runaway Dreams: The Story of Mama's Boys and Celtus* (Kennedy & Boyd). He is currently working on a monograph of Eric Bogle's songs/poems.

Thomas Kaffenberger received his Magister degree in Art History in 2011. Currently he is working on his PhD, entitled 'Tradition and Identity. Hagios Georgios in Famagusta and the Orthodox Ecclesiastical Architecture Under Lusignan, Genoese and Venetian Rule in Cyprus (14th–16th Century)', at Johannes Gutenberg University, Mainz and King's College London. He is working as a lecturer at the universities of Mainz and Heidelberg. In addition to several articles on Cypriot architecture, he has recently published the book *Lebensräume gestalten: Heinrich Metzendorf und die Reformarchitektur an der Bergstraße*, which deals with traditional concepts of architecture in the early twentieth century.

This paper explores a recent interdisciplinary project which brought together a visualization expert, an art historian, and an architectural historian, to study the ruins of Saint George of the Greeks Cathedral in Famagusta, eastern Cyprus, then create a virtual three-dimensional reconstruction of it. The motivation for this work, funded by Nanyang Technological University in Singapore, was to apply existing knowledge and expertise to a difficult, and very particular, heritage question on this Eastern Mediterranean Island. The creation of such a model could, it was felt, not only reiterate the academic value of thorough archival work married to state of the art technology, but also have very practical reverberations in terms of future heritage welfare and education via this 'borderless' domain.

The project objectives and a particular cultural dilemma

In June of 2012 a small pilot project began to survey and analyse the ruins of Saint George of the Greeks Cathedral in Famagusta, Cyprus, then create a three-dimensional virtual reconstruction of it. The motivation for this work, funded by Nanyang Technological University in Singapore, was not to set in motion further technical innovations as such, but to apply existing knowledge to a difficult, and very particular, heritage question. The creation of such a model could, it was felt, not only demonstrate the academic value of thorough archival work, but also have very practical reverberations in terms of heritage welfare, education and perhaps peace building. From the outset therefore, the authors would like to emphasise the holistic nature of this research project, its transient status and its wider social implications.

In order to understand the peculiarities of heritage issues in the northern part of Cyprus it is vital to situate our work within its socio-political context. In 1974, the island of Cyprus was forcibly divided by a military invasion that came at the end of a period of long-standing tension between Greek and Turkish nationalisms on the island. In 1983 the northern section of the island made permanent the partition by declaring its sovereign status as the 'Turkish Republic of Northern Cyprus'. This move was condemned by the United Nations and so to this day only Turkey formally recognises the existence of the 'nation' and its sovereignty. In 2014 this division still stands, despite a reunification effort which came very close to success in 2004 in the form of the United Nations proposed Annan Plan. As a result of the continued political impasse there is currently no international presence in the northern portion of the island that might deal with the complex cultural welfare and heritage management questions that have over the intervening decades become so urgent.

It was therefore to the 'borderless' virtual world that we turned our attention in 2012, as a domain or frontier for legal academic research. We targeted one single example, Saint George of the Greeks, as our pilot. The overall objectives of the interdisciplinary case study, undertaken by an art historian, an architectural historian and a computer visualisation expert, can be summarised as thus; to:

(1) *document* the endangered Cathedral of Saint George of the Greeks in Famagusta, Cyprus;
(2) *develop* techniques for visualisation and conservation projects using state-of-the-art technologies;
(3) *create* 3D modelling, GPS-sensitive, data recognition and visualisation methods to re-create historic spaces in a scholarly manner;
(4) *refine* educational methodologies for inculcating the importance of cultural heritage in future generations of schoolchildren in Famagusta (and further afield);
(5) *propose* to use 'shared' cultural heritage, in a 'neutral' space, as a method of political reconciliation between politically polar groups.

This paper, therefore, shares with the wider academic community the reasoning behind this project, the processes adopted and the findings to date, and highlights some of the academic objectives within the guidelines of the London Charter for computer-based visualisation of cultural heritage.[1]

Archives, manuscripts and historical research

It is vital to reiterate that this project, a work in progress, is not merely a technical exercise in what can and cannot be done using equipment and software; it is first and foremost an academic exercise into art and architectural history, whereby software and cutting-edge methodologies are created and adapted to assist in the original academic study. As such, creating a 3D representation of St George of the Greeks required a combination of technical knowledge of the building as well as a solid historical understanding of the landscape in which it sits. Of course, the most important material evidence was the remains of the building itself and so a thorough analysis and recording of what is extant today was undertaken. In addition to that, the team utilised almost 140 years of photographic sources from a vast array of collections and archives, ranging from Harvard University (Foscolo), the Courtauld Institute of Art (Conway), La Médiathèque de l'Architecture et du Patrimoine (Lucien Roy) to the National Archive of the United Kingdom (Kew). The unpublished Mogabgab Photographic Archive (currently in boxes in the Department of Antiquities in northern Nicosia), created in the 1930s–50s by the Director of Antiquities for Famagusta, is a particularly good source for understanding building details. Local archives, specifically those relating to the British period on the island, where vital clues can be gleaned from government reports (Report to the Department of Antiquities of Cyprus) relating to expenditure and permissions, were also vital. Going back to pre-photography years, we used the work of travelling artists and the journals of writers conducted almost continuously over the centuries, a fine example of which can be seen in the copperplate created by Cornelis de Bruyn in 1698 (see Figure 4).[2] We have leaned heavily too on the imagery derived from map-makers, including Sebastian Munster (1578), Simon Pinargenti (1572) and Stephano Gibellino (1571), Olfert Dapper (1688) and also on architectural models by Giovanni Sanmichele (circa 1540s) held in the Venice Museo Storico Navale. The main scholarly sources used for the project were the architectural studies of Camille Enlart (Enlart 1899), the works of George Jeffery, published throughout the first decades of the twentieth century,[3] and more recent research by Kaffenberger.[4] The 3D model of the historic structure, it is clear, utilises as many footnotes and references to archival and manuscript sources as any good journal article. Creating such an image in Singapore was only possible after long-term, trans-continental and multi-disciplinary work had been carried out.

Methodologies, interpretation and visualisation

A note on methodology here seems timely with the caveat that any attempt at reconstruction of a (partly) vanished artefact is prone to subjectivity (Figure 1). We pursued our work in the knowledge that at least three instances of subjectivity are distinguishable in the reconstruction process. A first instance lies within the source material: any source, apart from the sheer material evidence, is refracted by the perception of the original material of the person contributing to the source. The second instance occurs when the artefact and textual and pictorial sources are interpreted by a scholar, which again adds a certain amount of subjectivity, even though the output might be perceived as objective and proven. The third instance lies in the process of a reconstruction itself. Unlike a text, which refers only to a relatively well-demonstrated theory, a visualisation can be much more sweeping, especially in the traditional method of drawings and model making. To proceed with caution therefore was essential.

That said, the use of digital technologies to support the conservation of, and enhance the educational abilities pertaining to, cultural heritage by supplying new tools

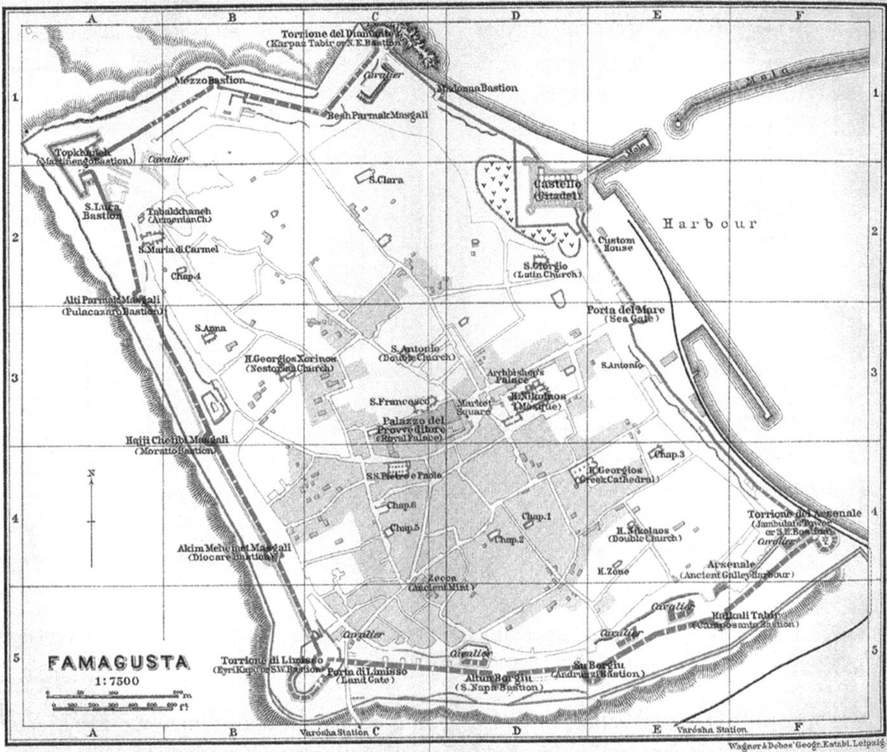

Figure 1. Map of Famagusta, circa 1917. Private collection, originally from Karl Baedeker, *Konstantinopel, Balkanstaaten, Kleinasien, Archipel, Cypern, Leipzig 1914.* 146×179mm.

for research and dissemination was the assumed starting point of this project. We also worked on the understanding that these digital technologies, through their capacity to create networks and re-create experience, might allow the scholar to foster a wider, better informed, more engaged audience. In addition to creating a snap-shot of how the cathedral looked in 2012, therefore, we felt that our 3D visualisation might foster, then enable, a sophisticated academic debate which would allow the virtual structure to be continually re-modelled based on emerging and contrasting research. We knew too that such 3D visualisations might offer experts the opportunity to analyse the durability of the structure and to prepare for the years ahead by mapping areas that are most at risk. In Famagusta this is an important task as historic monuments remain uninspected. A second advantage of the 3D model is that, whether utilised by a specialist scrutinising every detail or offering light entertainment to a virtual tourist in a distant location, Saint George of the Greeks can now be transported anywhere there is an Internet connection. As such, a huge awareness of what is in Famagusta (and endangered) has been created, as has the opportunity to 'visit' the site without actually physically walking over it and causing further destruction.[5] Additionally, the audience has been broadened to include classrooms, museums, heritage organisations and governments who otherwise may not have been aware of the existence of these heritage sites or the dangers they faced. The recent study on the Roman villa of Casa de Freiria in Spain (Rua and Alvito 2011), the iPad application 'Virtual History ROMA' (Arnoldo Mondadori Editore, SpA) and 'Chaos to Perfection' (Les 84 and ChateauVersailles 2012) are all testimonies to the

Figure 2. Hagios Georgios (right larger structure) and Hagios Epiphanios (left smaller structure), south-eastern facades. Photograph by Thomas Kaffenberger.

varying uses of 3D visualisation in conservation, education and immersive experience.[6] It is well understood that presenting the 'artefact' online can be achieved either by utilising the newly improved capabilities of HTML 5 and WebGL (and so making it available to most browsers),[7] or through the use of third-party plug-ins. In addition to screen-based media, educators are also turning to the use of physical computing and immersive experience as a means for sharing information and entertainment. By using a cave, for example, or augmented reality, users can experience the site as if they were standing inside it and so an experimental digital classroom project (Educube) is currently being tested at a school in Singapore. Here students could potentially experience a virtual classroom with interactive walls and touch screen interfaces as they learn 'within' Saint George of the Greeks. Just as one explores the rainforests of the Amazon, so too one can 'experience' the endangered art and architecture of Famagusta (Figure 2).

The Cathedral of St George of the Greeks

In its heyday Famagusta was one of the wealthiest cities in the medieval Mediterranean world and it was probably the coronation place of the Lusignan dynasty, which held the crown of both Cyprus and Jerusalem. It was also a city condemned for its hedonism by Saint Brigitte of Sweden, earmarked for destruction in Dante's *Inferno* and the setting for Shakespeare's tragedy *Othello*. Its end came in one of the most infamous sieges in military history (1571), after which it was entirely forgotten and, because of earthquake, plague and policy, abandoned for three centuries. Experiencing a degree of revitalisation under British administration (1878–1960), Famagusta's heritage was granted a brief reprieve, but this, for the reasons outlined in the opening section, was to be short-lived.

Amongst the many ruins and medieval structures within Famagusta Walled City, around 30 churches are preserved or traceable today. Saint George of the Greeks lies in

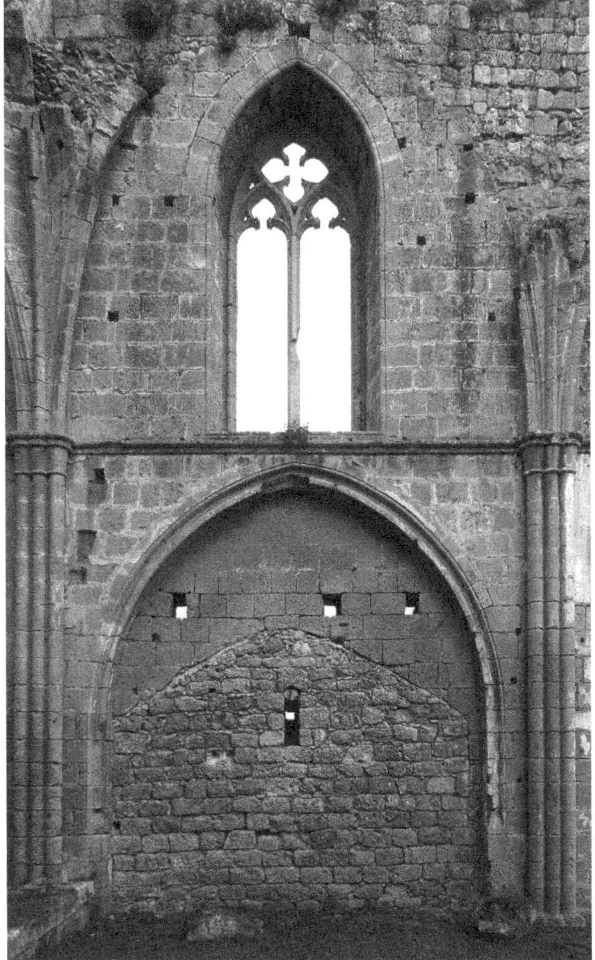

Figure 3. Southern wall (4th bay) of St George incorporating northern wall of the older Hagios Epiphanios. Photograph by Thomas Kaffenberger.

the south-east, some 100 metres south of the Latin Cathedral of Saint Nicholas, in the so-called Greek Quarter. Consisting of a much-altered older part, Hagios Epiphanios, and the monumental new cathedral erected in the fourteenth century, Hagios Georgios (Saint George), the complex demands the highest possible scholarly treatment.[8] Hagios Epiphanios, presumably functioning as a place of veneration of the island's most important saint bishop, originates in the Middle Byzantine era (around 1000 AD) and was renovated, rebuilt and extended at least five times. By the mid-fourteenth century the church was two-aisled and surmounted by four domes, yet compared to the newly erected Latin buildings in the city it was small in scale. Nevertheless, the old structure, thus functioning as material testimony of the bishopric's long tradition, was preserved during the erection of the splendid new cathedral of Hagios Georgios in the second half of the fourteenth century. The new structure, which incorporates the older building in its southern wall (Figure 3), now shows an elaborate blending of traditional Cypriot, Crusader Style and French Gothic elements.

Figure 4. Copperplate of Famagusta portraying St George of the Greeks with a dome, circa 1698, Cornelius de Bruyn. Private Collection.

It is made entirely of limestone ashlars and has three aisles of five bays each, all ending in semi-circular apses. While the apses, facade and aisle walls are plain, the basilical clerestory was supported by a row of flying buttresses, which held back the thrust of the cross vaults surmounting every bay. A long scholarly debate as to whether there was a dome or not was ended only recently by the uncovering of definitive evidence (Figure 4) in support of the notion.

Minor alterations to the church occurred in the fifteenth century, but the structure seems to have stayed intact until the Ottoman cannonade of 1571. In fact travellers' accounts and artists' impressions from the seventeenth century[9] show that while the cathedral was undoubtedly badly damaged in the siege of 1571, its final demise probably came in the great earthquake of 1735.[10] It was only after this point that Saint George of the Greeks was finally abandoned and remains a ruin to the present day (Figure 5).

Figure 5. East-facing interior of St George of the Greeks, 2012. Photograph by Sven J Norris.

Mainly intact are the three apses, the southern aisle wall and the lower storey of the facade, while the northern aisle wall, clerestory and the vaults (including piers) are mostly gone.[11] Rests of the cross vaults are visible in the Eastern bays, where also the last flying buttress gives support to the main apse semi-dome. Stones of the church have been removed over the centuries for building projects further afield (it has been suggested as far away as Egypt),[12] further collapse has occurred over time and, despite an intervention in the 1930s,[13] the once vibrant murals are now exposed to baking heat in the summer, the destructive effects of rainwater in the winter and neglect.

Platforms, reconstructions and limitations

In re-creating the structure, the modellers adopted two distinct methodologies which would later be combined. The first of these was a high resolution or polycount, which enabled photo-realistic rendered images or pre-rendered walkthroughs of the space in the form of video. This particular output and style of 3D modelling is most commonly found in architectural visualisation or set design for film production. The second was a low resolution or polycount version of the model, which enabled a real-time 3D engine to process the structure and permit a real-time navigable experience as is common with many 3D video games today, such as the *Assassin's Creed* series (Ubisoft Montreal, 2007–13), *Elder Scrolls: Skyrim* (Bethesda Game Studios, 2011) and *Dear Esther* (Briscoe, 2012). This low resolution method was the main goal in terms of creating the 3D model of St George of the Greeks and, while being light in terms of physical construction of the 3D mesh (a low polygon or face count), inherited textures rendered from the higher resolution model. The idea behind this, and indeed how many contemporary video games and real-time applications function, is that an aesthetically realistic environment or object can be presented to the viewer while the underlying physical structure of the model is in fact quite crude. A physical analogy of this might be a film or stage set which might be painted and dressed very accurately from the audience's point of view but is in fact just a facade made of scaffold and canvas behind the scenes.

Following the modelling of St George of the Greeks in 3D space, and in order to texture it, the image had to be unwrapped and given UVW coordinates which mapped the 3D object onto a 2D plane. This then allowed the painting and art manipulation of the object and specified where a 2D image should be projected on the 3D surface. A simple analogy is how the pelt of an animal appears once it has been skinned. Most 3D models in contemporary real-time environments are made up of a number of different textures which contain various image data used to project realism into a 3D surface. The most common textures used are: Diffuse Map (displays general colour and pattern); Normal Map (used by the game engine to give appearance of 3D depth on a flat surface); and Specular Map (affects the glossiness or matt appearance on the 3D object surface).

Figure 6 shows an example of the earliest initial setup in Autodesk 3D Studio Max, where the plan, sections and elevations (the latter of which are not shown) were placed to scale as visual aids for the modelling process. The building plan being used (Figure 7) is a modernised adaption of Theophilus Mogabgab's original plan while the cross-section was drawn by Camille Enlart in 1896 (Figure 8). It must be noted that all of these references varied by date, accuracy and interpretation.

This setup was used for the initial 'blocking in' of the structure, a process which can be compared to the initial sketches an artist makes before a final painting is produced. This procedure helps to identify major structures and components, while aiming

Figure 6. Screenshot of initial setup in Autodesk 3D Studio Max, 2012. Image by Sven J Norris.

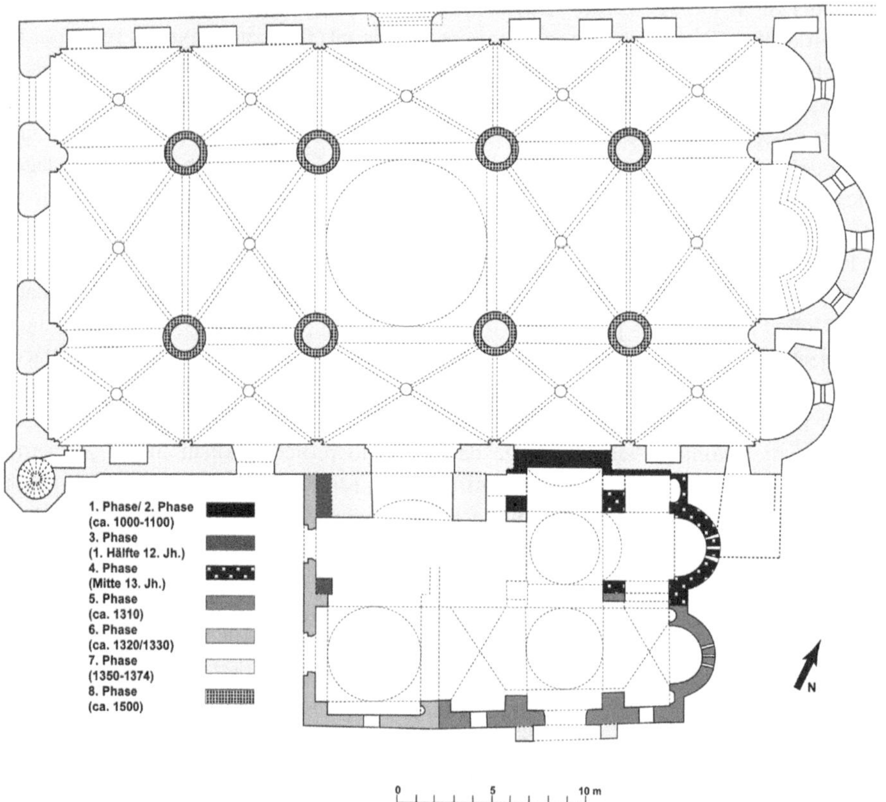

Figure 7. Plan of St George of the Greeks and Hagios Epiphanios. Plan by Thomas Kaffenberger.

Figure 8. East-facing section of St George of the Greeks, 1896. Illustration by Camille Enlart.

to capture the actual composition and scale of the building. For example, certain areas of the cathedral, such as windows, some vaults and arches, are repetitive and these were modelled once and then instanced.

The included example render from a recent but not final version (Figure 9) depicts both structures from a south-western orientation of the site showing St George with its roof intact, buttresses and a suggested dome which has since been modified. Figure 10 shows an early interior render of St George indicating a very different experience to the present-day roofless site.

As almost all of the interior decoration of the building has been eroded and destroyed over time, many of the original frescoes are lost forever and can therefore not be reconstructed accurately. The 3D model enables the possibility of at least displaying the existing remnants of frescoes within the interior.

Future trajectories

As well as photorealistic renders and walkthroughs of the buildings from any angle, the creation of a real-time 3D version has begun using the popular game engine Unity 3D. Embedded within this digital interface (for Web or tablet), the user will be able to access first-person control and bird's eye views of the structures both inside and out. In addition, much like a kiosk experience, contextual displays and interactive hotspots will enable the user to read information, hear audio and perhaps watch related video footage.

Figure 9. South-western sample render of the modelled structures (in progress), 2013. Image by Sven J Norris.

Figure 10. St George of the Greeks, early draft render of interior, 2013. Image by Sven J Norris.

To date we have generated the models showing the buildings as they may have been at a given moment in history. Next we would like to generate models (including the present-day situation) where users are able to switch between time periods dynamically, perhaps through the use of a chronological timeline slider or mechanism within the interface. As different phases of the building are added to the model, these can be incorporated into the chronological timeline mechanism.

Documentation remains a vital part of the process (and the progress) and as such, a Wordpress site has been set up. This 'wiki' can help to preserve the transparency of the development of the project, contribute to the sustainability of the work output and eventually be made public as part of a wider citizen science project.

Though the team does not wish to re-involve cultural heritage in the same political theatre that has been so detrimental to it, it is nevertheless interested in motivating communities to act together to safeguard heritage despite all other differences. Costa Carras, Vice-President of Europa Nostra, for example, underlined that 'culture can work as one of the creative forces in European society that brings people together.'[14] Michael Møller, the UN Chief of Mission on Cyprus, also emphasised his pleasure that such work in Famagusta would 'encourage the two communities to work together and, just as importantly, [of] encourage[ing] them to safeguard the common cultural heritage of Cyprus'.[15]

Lastly, might not the outcomes of this project, so easily disseminated worldwide, act as a lobbying tool for universities, non-government organisations and perhaps even governments to permit a return of scholarship and conservation expertise to a city that has been abandoned by the international community for too long? The reasoning was certainly endorsed by World Monuments Fund when they wrote:

> The scale of preserving the remaining historic elements of Famagusta is of such enormous proportions that one almost does not know where to begin. It is therefore of vital importance to increase the world's awareness of the special qualities of Famagusta and to lay the necessary ground work for an appropriate evolution of the city from an isolated gem to an accessible, well protected, historic, urban site.[16]

Perhaps our work has taken a first, small, step in that entirely necessary direction. Though there is still much to be done on the pilot study of St George of the Greeks, one's attention already turns to the wider implications of this successful experiment for each and every monument in Famagusta, or to the entire historic city as a 'heritage unit'. Allowing ourselves to widen our perspective further, might there even be positive ramifications for the other fragile heritage sites of the northern part of Cyprus as a whole, and indeed for the endangered heritage of other unrecognised 'states' worldwide? It seems that with the rapid development of visualisation technologies, anchored by solid academic research, there might now be room for optimism in terms of re-engaging international scholarship and engineering know-how with monuments previously deemed out of reach.

Endnotes

1. For a full text of the London Charter see 'The London Charter for the Computer-Based Visualisation of Cultural Heritage (Version 2.1, February 2009)', in *Paradata and Transparency in Virtual Heritage*, Drew Baker, Anna Bentkowska-Kafel and Hugh Denard (eds), Ashgate, Farnham, 2012, pp. 73–80.
2. Michael Walsh, '*Othello,* "Turning Turks" and Cornelis de Bruyn's Copperplate of the Ottoman Port of Famagusta in the Seventeenth Century', *Mariners Mirror*, November 2012, pp. 448–466.
3. C Enlart, *L'Art gothique et la Renaissance en Chypre*, vol 2, Nabu Press, Paris, 1899; English translation: D Hunt (trans) *Gothic Art and the Renaissance in Cyprus*, Trigraph, London, 1987. George Jeffery, 'The Orthodox Cathedral of Famagusta, Cyprus', *The Builder*, vol. 87, 1904, pp. 31–4; George Jeffery, 'Notes on Cyprus, 1905' *Journal of the Royal Institute of British Architects*, vol. 8, 1906, pp. 481–93; George Jeffery, 'The Byzantine Churches of Cyprus' *Proceedings of the Society of Antiquaries London*, vol. 28, 1916, pp. 111–34.
4. Thomas Kaffenberger, Harmonizing the Sources: An Insight into the Appearance of the Hagios Georgios Complex at Various Stages of Its Building History, forthcoming.
5. This kind of interference was evidenced by the recent documentary *Cave of Forgotten Dreams* (Werner Herzog, 2010).

6. H Rua and P Alvito (2011) 'Living the past: 3D models, virtual reality and game engines as tools for supporting archaeology and the reconstruction of cultural heritage - the case study of the Roman villa of Casal de Freiria', *Journal of Archaeological Science*, vol. 38, no. 12, 2011, pp. 3296 – 3308; Les 84 and Chateau Versailles, 'Chaos To Perfection - A tour of Versailles', 2012, available at <http.www.chaostoperfection.com>, accessed 10 September 2012.
7. French developers Les 84 in collaboration with Google Culture and Chateau de Versailles have already made a stand on the use of this kind of technology in order to bring a vibrant feel to cultural heritage and appreciation by creating *Chaos To Perfection* (Les 84 and ChateauVersailles 2012).
8. All information concerning the chronology of the building is presented as in Thomas Kaffenberger, *Harmonizing the Sources – Textual, Pictorial and Material Evidence Contributing to a New Insight Into the Construction History and Original Appearance of the Orthodox Episcopal Churches of Hagios Georgios and Hagios Epiphanios*, in *The Harbour of All This Sea and Realm: Crusader to Venetian Famagusta*, M Walsh, T Kiss and N Coureas (eds), CEU Press, Budapest, in press.
9. See Walsh.
10. The pilgrim Richard Pococke states in 1738: 'St George's, one of the most magnificent [churches], was thrown down by the earthquake.' For Pococke's full account see: Claude Delaval Cobham, *Excerpta Cypria. Materials for a History of Cyprus*, Cambridge University Press, Cambridge, 1908, pp. 251–70.
11. For a more immersive view of the present-day structure, a 360-degree panorama can be viewed at *<http://360.io/Gv92Mj>*, created 26 June 2012.
12. Elizabeth Hoak-Doering 'Stones of the Suez Canal: A Discourse of Absence and Power in Cyprus and Egypt', *Journal of Balkan and Near Eastern Studies*, vol. 14, no. 2, 2012, pp. 199–228; M Walsh, '"On of the princypalle Havenes of the See": The Port of Famagusta and the Ship Graffiti of Its Ruined Churches', *International Journal of Nautical Archaeology*, vol. 37, no. 1, 2008, pp. 115–129; M Walsh, '"The Vile Embroidery of Ruin": Historic Famagusta between Ottoman and British Empires in *Fin de Siècle* Cyprus: 1878–1901', *Journal of Intercultural Studies*, vol. 31, no. 3, 2010, pp. 247–269.
13. The works were initiated by Theophilus Mogabgab, head of the Department of Antiquities at that time. Theophilus Mogabgab, 'Excavations in Famagusta', *Report to the Department of Antiquities Cyprus* 1935 (1936), pp. 20–22; Theophilus Mogabgab, 'Excavations and Improvements in Famagusta', *Report to the Department of Antiquities Cyprus*, 1936/II (1939), pp. 103–105; Theophilus Mogabgab, 'Excavations and Researches in Famagusta 1937–1939', *RDAC*, 1937/1939 (1951), pp. 181–90.
14. Private communication between Carras and Walsh.
15. Private communication between Møller and Walsh.
16. R Silman and K Severson, *The Historic Walled City of Famagusta*, World Monuments Fund, New York City, 2008.

Digital archives and metadata as critical infrastructure to keep community memory safe for the future – lessons from Japanese activities

Shigeo Sugimoto

Shigeo Sugimoto received BE, ME and PhD degrees from the Department of Information Science, Faculty of Engineering, Kyoto University in 1977, 1979, and 1985, respectively. He joined the University of Library and Information Science (ULIS), Tsukuba, Japan in 1983. After the merger of ULIS with the University of Tsukuba, he has been teaching at the Graduate School of Library, Information and Media Studies, University of Tsukuba. He is a professor at the Faculty of Library, Information and Media Science, University of Tsukuba and currently a director of the Research Centre for Knowledge Communities, University of Tsukuba.

This paper discusses some key issues for digital archives and metadata in a networked information environment to keep our community memory for the future. The paper is based primarily on the experiences and lessons learnt by the author from his research activities on metadata and digital archives. The author participated in a study group on digital archives hosted by the Ministry of Internal Affairs and Communications of the Japanese Government from February 2011 to March 2012. The group discussed the promotion of digital archives in Japan, particularly at memory institutions. The Great East Japan Earthquake of 11 March 2011 caused serious damage in the north-eastern part of Japan, especially the Pacific coastal regions. This disaster significantly affected the discussions of the group. The basic lesson that the author learned is that digital archives built on a robust information environment are essential for keeping our community memory safe for the future. Not only do the primary digital resources need to be properly maintained and preserved for the future but also secondary resources, metadata and meta-metadata. We need to use Linked Open Data technologies to enhance the usability of such digital resources in the archives.

Introduction

A digital archive is a collection of digital resources maintained for long-term use. Many digital archives have been developed and are being used in our networked information society. Digital archives are built in many different places – not only in cultural fields but also in the science, technology, medical and social fields. Memory institutions – museums, libraries and archives – are key players when building and maintaining digital archives and providing them to users in many different communities today and in to the future. Digital archives are recognised as an important part of the knowledge and information infrastructure in our networked information society. They provide users with inexpensive access to valuable knowledge resources, which is crucial for a democratic society.

This paper aims to discuss a few key issues with respect to digital archives and metadata. It presents some basic issues and models of digital archives and metadata learnt from the author's digital archive research activities. The paper is primarily aimed at identifying and sharing issues with digital archives as a critical infrastructure for the safekeeping of the memory of our communities and societies.

The rest of this paper is organised as follows: section 2 describes the basic concepts of digital archives and discusses some related activities, section 3 presents the author's committee activities in Japan, section 4 discusses metadata issues for digital archives, in particular from the viewpoint of interoperability, section 5 introduces the digital archives of the Great East Japan Earthquake of March 2011, section 6 presents a few studies on metadata and digital archives at the author's laboratory and section 7 concludes this paper.

Digital archives – basic concepts and related works

Digital archive, in this paper, means a collection of digital resources selected, collected, organised and maintained for long-term use. This is a comprehensive definition of digital archive designed to include different types of digital collections, that is, from very high-technology oriented to off-the-shelf technology oriented, from cultural heritage to science resources and so on. Thus, the meaning of the term is not limited to a digitally archived collection of governmental records. Another term which has a meaning close to digital archive is digital curation. This paper uses these two terms with the same meaning. Another point which should be mentioned is that this paper does not distinguish between digital resources that are born-digital or digitised from non-digital.

The trend towards Open Data and Linked Open Data (LOD) is a crucial issue for the development of digital archives. Once a dataset is open, it is linked and used in combination with other resources by third parties. Digital archives should be open and linkable to each other to enhance their usability and to add value to the archived contents. Metadata is always key for the enhancement.

Memory institutions and governments have been playing important roles in building digital archives. In North America, American Memory at the US Library of Congress has more than 20 years' history of the development of large digital collections of cultural resources, and the Digital Public Library of America provides a broad range of resources. Europeana is a huge international collaborative project in Europe and its strength is not only in international collaboration but also in the use of LOD technologies for value addition by third parties.[1] In Asia, there are many digital archive projects as well. The Taiwan e-Learning and Digital Archives Program (TELDAP) is a good example of the use of digital archives in education.

Disasters, which may be caused by nature or by humans and may be large or regional, affect our lives and societies. On one hand, disasters are one of the major risks for valuable cultural resources of communities. On the other hand, memories and records about the disasters are also an important asset for the communities. Digital archives have a crucial role in keeping memories of disasters for the future.[2] In Japan, there are several archives that record the Great East Japan Earthquake which are described later in this paper. Community memory resources may, however, be destroyed by disasters which happen slowly, for example climate change and social changes of aging communities.

The Digital Curation Centre in the UK fosters long-term use of digital resources and their collections. Digital preservation and the longevity of digital resources are obviously important for digital archives. More importantly, longevity adds value to the resources and archives.[3] Longevity of digital resources has been discussed since the 1990s. The risks of digital preservation have been discussed mainly from technological and/or management viewpoints. Longevity of metadata is a crucial aspect for digital archives as well as longevity of primary resources in digital formats, because we lose important handles to access and render the resources if their metadata is lost. Longevity of meta-metadata, which is metadata about metadata, is key to keeping metadata understandable and usable over time. Therefore, registries to keep information about metadata and archives are crucial. For example, the UK National Archives built a registry service named PRONOM to keep information about file formats.[4]

Provenance of resources is recognised as critical information for digital preservation as provenance is one of four main categories of Preservation Description Information of the Open Archival Information System.[5] The World Wide Web consortium has proposed a model to describe provenance which is not specifically designed for digital archiving but gives us a generalised model for provenance description.[6] Metadata provenance is also crucial to track changes in metadata schemas as well as mappings among metadata vocabularies. Metadata provenance description is meta-metadata because it is a description of metadata. Eckert and colleagues reported a model for meta-metadata based on the Resource Description Framework (RDF).[7] In general, preservation of metadata as a document would not be as complicated as preservation of computer games because metadata is described as textual data. However, the requirement to keep track of semantic changes of metadata and meta-metadata in a machine-interpretable form presents a challenge.

Open Data and Linked Open Data are very important movements for memory institutions and related communities. Governments are making an effort to make governmental resources open and usable for the public in order to add more value to their data. LOD is a crucial movement to link data available on the Web by semantic links.[8] Europeana, for example, is a large-scale application of LOD. Federated search has been a common function among digital archives. However, those digital archives participating in the federated search have to agree on a protocol and metadata schema for search in advance, that is, semi-open data. LOD provides us with a less tightly connected model for resource access across different archives. Thus, it is crucial to link digital archives by semantic links based on LOD across communities and over time.

Digital archives of memory institutions in Japan

Overview of digital archives

In Japan, the National Diet Library (NDL), the Agency for Cultural Affairs (ACA) under the Ministry of Education, Culture, Sports, Science and Technology, and the National Archives of Japan (NAJ) have been developing large digital archives – for example, the Digital Library of Books published in the Meiji era and early twentieth century by NDL.[9] NDL has a wealth of experience in developing digital archives and federated search services,[10] Cultural Heritage Online (CHO) by the ACA and National Institute of Informatics (NII),[11] and the digital collection of government records covering the period from after the revolution in the nineteenth century to World War II by the Japan Center for Asian Historical Records at NAJ.[12] NII is a national hub for scholarly information that provides CiNii as a portal to scholarly information resources.[13]

Some university and regional public memory institutions have been working on digitisation of their holdings and regional heritage. National museums have also developed digital collections of their holdings. For university libraries, digitisation of cultural heritage is not a central service but they have been keenly working on electronic journal services and institutional repositories. Some national museums have produced digital collections and collaborated with ACA for the development of CHO. On the other hand, digitisation activities of the regional memory institutions, ie, Museums, Libraries and Archives (MLA), are still limited.

The disaster caused by the great earthquake and tsunami on 11 March 2011 was recorded by many people using digital devices. MIC, NDL, Tohoku University,[14] Harvard Reischauer Center[15] and other partners have been collaborating to collect digital resources to build a digital archive of the disaster. NDL, as the hub of the partners, opened Hinagiku, the digital archive of the disaster, in March 2013.[16] Hinagiku works as a portal to the participating digital archives. The experience at Kobe University Library in building their disaster archive for the earthquake that happened in January 1995 helped the recent archiving activity.

Archiving is an ongoing task. Digital archives for a major disaster play an important role from many viewpoints – information resources for governments to build their risk management plans; scholarly resources for researchers in many fields such as civil engineering, social risk management, risk management technologies, history and sociology; educational resources at many levels; and community memory resources for people in regional communities. An important challenge for a disaster archive is to enhance the usability of archived resources for the general public across communities, for example reference services using the disaster archives, and help for people and communities to record their personal or local memories of the disaster.

MIC Study Group on Digital Archives and NDL Roundtable on Digital Information Resources

The Ministry of Internal Affairs and Communications (MIC) hosted a study group from February 2011 to March 2012 to discuss issues in the promotion of digital archives of MLAs.[17] The author participated in the group as its chairperson. The NDL hosted a Roundtable on Digital Information Resources to discuss issues in the promotion of the collection and use of digital information resources, including the promotion of collaboration among MLAs. The roundtable started in 2010 and ended in 2012.

Both groups shared concerns about the development of digital archives in Japan, particularly developments at regional MLAs. MLA collaboration was a main topic of the NDL roundtable. NAJ have been developing their digital archives as a core function. On the other hand, digitisation at national museums and their metadata exchange with other institutions are less visible. There is a common understanding that MLA collaboration is crucial to promote use of heritage resources. Connecting resources stored at different institutions is vital for MLA collaboration, which means that metadata sharing is key to connecting the resources of MLAs. However, metadata sharing among MLAs is still limited because there is no well-recognised standard and limited development of shareable metadata at museums. Another issue shared among the participants was the accessibility of museum resource information via the Internet.

Discussions at the MIC Study Group

The group first agreed that MLAs, especially those founded by regional governments, are facing common barriers such as a lack of human resources and insufficient IT skills and experience. Longevity of digital resources is also a common concern for memory institutions when investing their precious funds.

The great earthquake happened on 11 March 2011, soon after the first meeting of the MIC Study Group. The disaster significantly affected the discussions of this study group. Many MLAs facing the Pacific coast were seriously damaged by the tsunami. Many rescue activities were carried out but it was not possible to perfectly recover the damaged resources. The situation in the area affected by the nuclear plant accident was much worse. Because people had to move out of the affected area, rescue activity soon after the disaster was not possible and continuity of the regional community was threatened.

The study group agreed that promotion of digital archives is a key strategy for MLAs aiming to keep their community memory safe from disasters and changes to social environments, in spite of arguments of lack of longevity of digital resources compared with physical resources. What the author learnt from this discussion is that physical things are easily lost in disasters and digital resources properly stored and backed up are more robust against disasters. Another important point agreed by the study group is that it is crucial to create and maintain metadata of resources to make them usable also in the networked environment. This means that it is important to maintain information about metadata, that is, meta-metadata and metadata schema. Thus, we agreed to understand the problems in a layered view – collection building, maintenance and provision of access to digital resources, data storage and preservation to share the digital resources, metadata storage and sharing to share information about the digital resources, and meta-metadata storage and sharing to share information about metadata.

Digital preservation is obviously critical for the longevity of digital archives. It is necessary to reduce both the risk of loss of contents and costs of preservation in both financial and environmental respects. The most fundamental issue for a memory institution is to establish its preservation policies and a maintenance system for preserved resources. Sharing an archiving infrastructure looks reasonable but the different requirements of memory institutions can make it difficult.

The final report of the study group recommends the promotion of the following four principles. These are primarily agreed for the development of digital archives at small- and medium-scale MLAs.

(1) enhance open access to resources at memory institutions – moving from paper-based management to digital resource management;
(2) develop human resource development infrastructure;
(3) develop system and service infrastructure;
(4) develop metadata information-sharing infrastructure.

Library information services are fairly well standardised and provided via the Internet. However, the management of resource information at museums is, in general, not as well standardised as library resource information because of the diversity of collections. Providing information about museum holdings via the Internet enormously improves the accessibility to those resources. Human resource development is a necessity for regional MLAs developing digital collections and improving their services via the Internet. The report recommends building a network of people and organisations to help MLAs develop their human resources. The report also recommends building a cloud environment for MLAs. For museums, the report encourages the use of Cultural Heritage Online as their shared infrastructure to make their heritage resources visible on the Internet. The group also agree that the Linked Open Data movement is crucial to improving accessibility and usability of digital archives. As an example of good practice, the group discussed the LODAC museum project hosted at NII, which is collecting information resources from museum sites using LOD technology.[18] The report recommends using URIs to identify every resource and to adopt the International Standard Identifier of Libraries and Related Organisations (ISIL, ISO 15511:2009) as the base identification scheme. The group agreed that sharing metadata information is crucial to enhancing metadata interoperability. A fundamental service for metadata information sharing is metadata schema registries that suit the Web, particularly LOD environments. Another key issue in sharing metadata is the rights statements about the metadata, a kind of meta-metadata.

Metadata issues for digital archives

Interoperability – Dublin Core-based view

Metadata interoperability is a key issue for digital archives in two respects – interoperability across domains and over time. The Dublin Core Application Profile (DCAP) is an important framework for metadata interoperability.[19] DCAP splits structural features and semantic components of metadata to define interoperable metadata across domains. In order to enhance semantic interoperability among the metadata schemas, DCAP suggests metadata schema designers use existing terms rather than define new terms because metadata vocabularies are the principal semantic basis of the metadata. Formal schemes to share metadata schemas are necessary for better metadata interoperability. Both the RDF and the Web Ontology Language (OWL) are important standards for metadata schema.

Meta-metadata – a generalised view for metadata interoperability

Metadata is defined as '(structured) data about data'. There is a data about a metadata, that is, meta-metadata, meta-meta-metadata and so forth. The 1-to-1 (one-to-one) principle of Dublin Core, which says one metadata for one instance, is a simple and crucial model for understanding the importance of meta-metadata.

Let us take a catalogue record of a book as an example. The record is eventually updated and the processing history is recorded. The update information and processing history is metadata of a catalogue record. This metadata is crucial for catalogue management but is not metadata of any book. As a catalogue record is metadata of a book, metadata about the catalogue record is meta-metadata of the book. Learning Object Metadata (LOM), for example, has a category named meta-metadata, which includes attributes for management of metadata. For another example, provenance description of metadata of a preserved resource is meta-metadata of the preserved resource. Thus, provenance information of metadata of a preserved resource is important as well as provenance information of the preserved resource.

Longevity of metadata schemas

Longevity of metadata schemas involves both semantics and infrastructure. A basic semantic problem is the change of meanings of metadata terms over time, namely the semantic drift of words and phrases. Another is the longevity of identification schemes for identifying metadata terms, vocabularies and schemas.

An obvious solution from the semantic perspective is to preserve metadata vocabulary definitions as a document. A metadata schema registry described in the next section is an efficient tool to maintain metadata vocabularies over time and across communities. It is necessary for the long-term maintenance of metadata to include appropriate references to the preserved metadata vocabularies from metadata schemas, that is, metadata for metadata schemas. Standardised metadata schemas and their vocabularies are maintained by maintenance agencies of metadata standards. Unfortunately, not all maintenance agencies live forever, so there is a risk that community-based metadata vocabulary documents will be lost over time. Keeping metadata schema information in a registry trusted and shared among the communities would be a simple solution.

URIs are the base identification scheme of resources on the Web. Each URI is an identifier of a corresponding metadata term or a resource. All of these links should be maintained over time but it is not easy to preserve links consistently because domain names are not persistent.

Metadata schema registry – a crucial service for metadata schema sharing across communities and over time

A metadata schema registry (or simply metadata registry) is a service to store metadata schemas and their components and to provide them on the Internet.[20] The primary instances stored in a registry are metadata vocabularies, that is, terms which represent metadata attributes, value classes and so on. On the Internet, both humans and machines use metadata, which means that every metadata term should be properly labelled for humans and, at the same time, should be given a unique identifier for machines. Therefore, proper localisation of metadata labels, and management and maintenance of URIs of metadata terms are the fundamental requirements for metadata interoperability across communities and over time.

The Open Metadata Registry[21] provides a rich set of metadata terms. Schema.org[22] and Linked Open Vocabulary[23] also provide rich sets of metadata vocabularies. The author has been involved in the development of two registries – DCMI Metadata Registry[24] and MetaBridge.[25] Both provide metadata schemas in RDF. MetaBridge stores not only metadata vocabularies but also description set profiles.

Digital archives and disaster – some lessons learnt

Great East Japan Earthquake digital archive

Memory institutions are responsible for keeping our memory for the future. As mentioned in a previous section, there are large digital archiving efforts led by the Japanese government to record the disaster and keep community memories into the future. Hinagiku at NDL, launched for public access in March 2013, is based on the collaboration of many public and private sectors – universities, libraries, regional and national broadcasting stations, newspaper companies, IT companies, local communities and so forth. NDL, Tohoku University and other partners have been collecting the resources and are continuing their efforts. An important issue for these archiving efforts is to get broader interest and higher recognition among the general public.

Hinagiku works as a search portal to access many databases – 29 participating databases including 16 databases dedicated to the East Japan Earthquake. These participating databases are organised by different types of organisations – university libraries, regional public libraries, newspaper and broadcasting companies, regional public sectors and Non-Profit Organisations, and so forth.

In-depth discussions on some crucial issues are required to further develop the services such as pictures which contain private content and shocking scenes, secondary use of archived resources, reference services provided by regional memory institutions for regional people using archived resources, and so forth. A crucial issue for Hinagiku is the promotion of its use by those people living in the area and seriously affected by the disaster to keep their memories for the future and to help them recover from the disaster. Regional needs and nationwide needs are sometimes hard to satisfy at the same time. For example, terms and phrases used in regional communities are useful for regional people keeping their memories in the archive but are not always easy to understand for other users. The issue left for future research and development is to extend the functionality of the digital archives from preservation-and-access to linking people via the archived resources in order to help them keep their community memories.

The power of cloud and crowd

Regional government offices, museums, libraries and cultural heritage sites facing the Pacific coast were seriously damaged in the disaster. Physical objects were lost or damaged. Loss of metadata, for example catalogue records and provenance information, caused great difficulties for recovery of objects found after the disaster. An obvious conclusion from this experience is that physical objects are easily lost and digital copies of important resources should be stored in a robust environment to avoid the loss of memory.

Disasters on that scale do not happen frequently. However, smaller disasters, which do happen more frequently, also cause serious damage to the memories and records of regional communities. Environmental and social changes may cause serious damage, which may happen slowly but can be serious. There are arguments about the longevity of digital media and the costs of digitisation but the author considers that digital archiving is a solution for keeping community memory resources safe for the future regardless of the resource types – born-digital or non-digital, tangible or intangible. An important lesson is that institutions and communities that cannot afford digital archives should share a trusted repository to keep their memories safe.

Loss of metadata causes serious problems. Once metadata of an object is lost, it is very expensive to recover the metadata even if the archived object is kept safe or rescued. It is particularly hard to recover contextual information such as provenance, classification and value descriptions of the archived object. The intellectual power of humans is essential for recovering or adding contextual information. Crowdsourcing technology and practices would be one way to solve this problem. Morishima and colleagues presented a platform for crowdsourcing that applies human intelligence to semantic micro-tasks on a logical framework for artificial intelligence which is designed to cope with a large volume of data.[26] They apply the platform to track the running paths of tornadoes and to correct semantic errors in the bibliographic data of NDL. In the former example, it is easy for regional people to identify the location where a photo of a tornado is taken but very hard to automatically find the location. On the other hand, it is easy for computers to merge many data created by people into a database.

Linking digital resources across communities and over time

Linking born-digital resources on the Web

Electronic books are important new cultural resources. In traditional print publishing, electronic catalogue records of books are created separately from the books. However, in the electronic publishing environment, both book contents and catalogue records are realised as a digital instance and distributed on the Internet and Web. On the other hand, video and audio resources are also in a digital format and broadcasting stations broadcast their programs in a digital format. Thus, the borders separating books, video and audio are diminishing in the digital and networked environment. In the conventional print-centric publishing and analogue broadcasting environment, metadata is created separately from the primary resources, for example books and TV programs and their catalogue data. However, in the digital environment, metadata could be encoded and embedded within the primary resources. In the digital environment, the border between archived and non-archived resources is unclear because both resources are stored in a database and served over the Internet.

Linked Open Data has a large potential for the development of digital archives in the open community. Metadata embedded in a resource works as a link connecting resources. Those metadata semantically link resources. On one hand, those semantic links will add value to the digital archives; on the other hand, maintaining the semantics of links as well as maintaining links is a new research issue.

A cloud-based model for digital preservation

The preservation of digital objects is a crucial function for digital archives. Preserved objects may have longer lives than the archival systems where they were born. Cloud environments have potential for MLAs as robust environments to keep and share digital resources. The hierarchical layered model based on the layered model of cloud computing is worth discussing because it clarifies the layers of services – from domain-neutral services in the base layers to domain-specific services in the application layers.

The variety of digital objects is always increasing because the variety of devices and digitally published resources is always increasing, for example smart phones, tablet PCs, electronic books and games. In addition, metadata which describe intellectual, logical and physical features of every digital object have to be preserved with the object. The variety of metadata schemas is always increasing. Thus, memory institutions have a demand to store a large variety of digital objects in accordance with their own requirements, which is likely to increase the complexity of any digital preservation. The layered model shown in Figure 1 contains an additional layer that bridges the application-specific requirements and an application-neutral preservation system based on the Open Archival Information System (OAIS).

Cloud computing is a natural place for small memory institutions to implement their digital archives. A cloud computing environment is defined as a layered architecture, for example as Infrastructure as a Service (IaaS) and Software as a Service (SaaS). Hiding detailed information defined in lower layers is a primary function of the layered architecture. On the other hand, because 'packaging' is a central idea of OAIS we need to re-define 'packaging' suitable for a layered architecture of cloud computing. Askhoj and colleagues showed a layered model for preservation in the cloud environment where a layer for preservation is defined between an application service layer and a platform layer.[27] It maps entities in the OAIS reference model into the layered model.

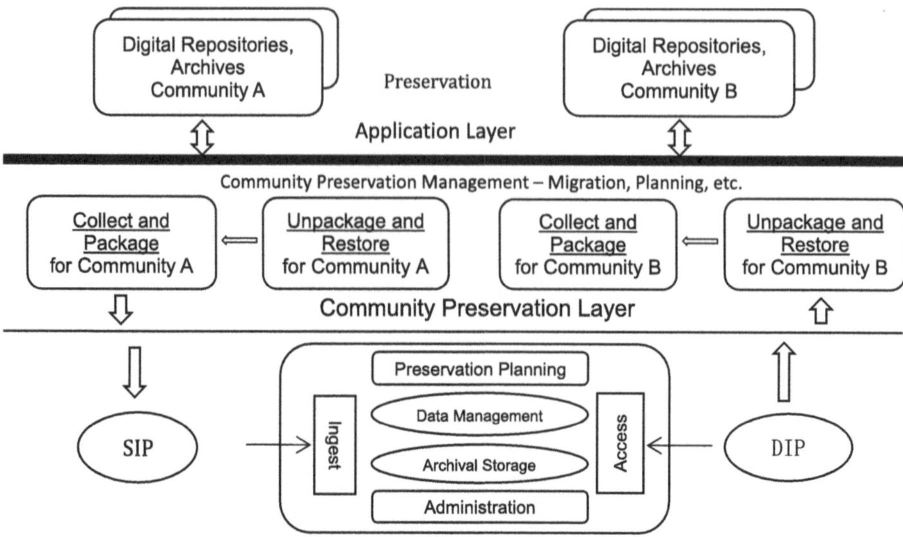

Figure 1. OAIS and layered model.

Discussion and concluding remarks

Digital archives are essential for our communities to keep our memory safe for the future. Metadata is key for the longevity of digital resources and digital archives. Longevity of archived resources is a primary concern of memory institutions. Physical entities are easily lost. The loss is caused not only by natural disasters but also by human activities. There are many arguments about the longevity of digital resources because of rapid technological changes. Longevity is primarily a management and policy issue rather than a technology issue.

A cloud computing environment has great potential for memory institutions building scalable and trusted digital archives because those institutions can use computation and storage power without worrying about human resources for maintaining computer systems. On the other hand, semantic information, which only humans can create, is crucial for memory institutions organising and providing information resources. Therefore, combining human intelligence and machine intelligence is necessary for the further progress of digital archives.

The development of electronic books and publishing industries will affect the organisation of digital collections and their archives. An important point in both the digital publishing and archiving environments is that any instance described in metadata can be a digital instance identified by a URI, so that any instance can be linked to other instances. Metadata and meta-metadata are also first-class instances as well as digital books and images. LOD technologies are obviously crucial for memory institutions to handle networked resources.

There is consensus that digital archiving is important for memory institutions regardless of their size. The lesson learnt from the great disaster of 11 March 2011 is that it is crucial to have securely stored digital copies, if we are to keep cultural heritage and memories of a community safe for the future. We also learnt that a lack or loss of metadata caused further damage to community memory.

Another lesson is the necessity of infrastructure to share metadata in order to improve the interoperability of our digital archives. RDF and LOD augment semantic linkage among the information resources on the Internet. Sharing metadata terms is a good way to improve semantic interoperability of metadata. Metadata schema registries that store and provide metadata terms enable semantic interoperability of metadata terms. Metadata interoperability over time is as important an issue as interoperability across communities. Preservation of both metadata and metadata terms is fundamental to keeping digital contents usable. However, current metadata schema preservation is not perfect.

Communities need information environments customised to their needs. Communities need information environments shared with other communities for information sharing and cost-saving. Thus, both specialisation for each community and generalisation among communities are required for community digital archives. We need not only good technologies but also good management practices and policies to solve these contradictions.

Acknowledgements

This study is supported in part by a Japan Society for Promotion of Sciences Grants-in-Aid for Scientific Research #22240023 and #25540153.

Notes

1. Europeana homepage, available at <*http://europeana.eu/*>, accessed February 2014.
2. Crisis, Tragedy, and Recovery Network, available at <*http://www.ctrnet.net/*>, accessed February 2014.
3. Digital Curation Centre, available at <*http://www.dcc.ac.uk/*>, accessed February 2014.
4. The National Archives, 'The Technical Registry PRONOM', available at <*http://www.nationalarchives.gov.uk/PRONOM/*>, accessed February 2014.
5. Consultative Committee for Space Data Systems (CCSDS), 'Reference Model for an Open Archival Information System Blue Book', June 2012, available at <*http://public.ccsds.org/publications/archive/650x0m2.pdf*>, accessed February 2014.
6. W3C Working Group Note, 'PROV Model Primer', 30 April 2013, available at <*http://www.w3.org/TR/prov-primer/*>, accessed February 2014.
7. K Eckert, M Pfeffer and H Stuckenschmidt, 'A Unified Approach for Representing Meta-metadata', in *Proceedings of International Conference on Dublin Core and Metadata Applications,* 2009, pp. 21–9, available at <*http://dcpapers.dublincore.org/pubs/article/view/973*>, accessed February 2014.
8. World Wide Web Consortium, 'Data – W3C', available at <*http://www.w3.org/standards/semanticweb/data*>, accessed February 2014.
9. National Diet Library, Digital Library From Meiji Era, available at <*http://kindai.ndl.go.jp/?__lang=en*>, accessed February 2014.
10. National Diet Library, 'List of Online Services', available at <*http://www.ndl.go.jp/en/service/online_service.html*>, accessed February 2014.
11. Cultural Heritage Online, available at <*http://bunka.nii.ac.jp/Index.do*>, accessed February 2014.
12. Japan Center for Asian Historical Records, available at <*http://www.jacar.go.jp/english/index.html*>, accessed February 2014.
13. National Institute of Informatics, 'CiNii', available at <*http://ci.nii.ac.jp/en*>, accessed February 2014.
14. Tohoku University, 'Michinoku Shinrokuden Archive', available at <*http://shinrokuden.irides.tohoku.ac.jp/*>, (in Japanese), accessed February 2014.
15. Harvard University, 'Digital Archive of Japan's 2011 Disasters', available at <*http://jdarchive.org/en/home*>, accessed February 2014.

16. National Diet Library, 'NDL Great East Japan Earthquake Archive', 2013, available at <*http://kn.ndl.go.jp/node?language=en*>, accessed February 2014.
17. Ministry of Internal Affairs and Communications, 'Expansion of Social Knowledge Infrastructure Through Digital Archive of Knowledge: Public Announcement of Proposal and Guidelines', 30 March 2013, available at <*http://www.soumu.go.jp/main_sosiki/joho_tsusin/eng/Releases/Telecommunications/120330_06.html*>, accessed February 2014.
18. LODAC, 'Linked Open Data for Academia', 2013, available at <*http://lod.ac/*>, accessed February 2014.
19. Dublin Core Metadata Initiative, 'The Singapore Framework of Dublin Core Application Profiles', 14 January 2008, available at <*http://dublincore.org/documents/singapore-framework/*>, accessed February 2014.
20. 'ISO 11179: Part 1, Framework', 18 November 2013, available at <*http://metadata-standards.org/11179/*>, accessed February 2014.
21. 'Open Metadata Registry', available at <*http://metadataregistry.org/*>, accessed February 2014.
22. Schema.org, available at <*http://schema.org/*>, accessed February 2014.
23. Pierre-Yves Vandenbussche, 'Linked Open Vocabularies (LOV)', available at <*http://lov.okfn.org/dataset/lov/*>, accessed February 2014.
24. DCMI Registry, 'The Dublin Core Metadata Registry', 2013, available at <*http://dcmi.kc.tsukuba.ac.jp/dcregistry/*>, accessed February 2014.
25. MetaBridge, 'About MetaBridge', available at <*https://www.metabridge.jp/infolib/metabridge/menu/?lang=en*>, accessed February 2014.
26. A Morishima, N Shinagawa, T Mitsuishi, H Aoki and S Fukusumi, 'CyLog/Crowd4U: A Declarative Platform for Complex Data-Centric Crowdsourcing', *Proceedings of VLDB Endowment*, vol. 5, no. 12, 2012, pp. 1918–21.
27. J Askhoj, S Sugimoto and M Nagamori, 'A Metadata Framework for Cloud-Based Digital Archives Using METS with PREMIS', in *Proceedings of ICADL 2011 Digital Libraries: For Cultural Heritage, Knowledge Dissemination, and Future Creation, Lecture Notes in Computer Science*, vol. 7008, 2011, pp. 118–27. J Askhoj, S Sugimoto and M Nagamori, 'Preserving Metadata in a Cloud', *Records Management Journal, Emerald*, vol. 21, no. 3, 2011, pp. 175–87.

Collecting the easily missed stories: digital participatory microhistory and the South Asian American Digital Archive

Michelle Caswell and Samip Mallick

Michelle Caswell is Assistant Professor of Archival Studies in the Department of Information Studies at UCLA and a co-founder and board member of the South Asian American Digital Archive. She is the author of Archiving the Unspeakable: Silence, Memory, and the Photographic Record in Cambodia, as well as numerous articles in Archival Science, American Archivist, Archivaria.

Samip Mallick is the executive director and co-founder of the South Asian American Digital Archive.

This paper defines and delineates the concept of participatory microhistory through an examination of the South Asian American Digital Archive's First Days Project, a community-based online project that solicits short audio, video and written narratives about South Asians immigrants' first day in the United States. First, this paper provides a brief overview of the history of the South Asian American Digital Archive and the First Days Project. Next, this paper highlights three important functions filled by participatory microhistory projects: they generate new records that represent perspectives not commonly found in archives, they convey an important sense of emotion and affect, and they effectively solicit community participation in the archival endeavour. Throughout, this paper explores participatory microhistory projects as tools to harness technology for community empowerment and build support for archives.

> *A first day is so much more than just one day.* The first day in a new country can be full of excitement, nervousness, loss, humor, sadness, anticipation, confusion, and a mixture of many other emotions. One day can encapsulate both what has come before and anticipate what will come after.[1]

Thus begins the introduction to the First Days Project, a community-based online project that solicits brief audio, video and written narratives about South Asian immigrants' first day in the United States. The project is run by the South Asian American Digital Archive (SAADA) (<*http://www.saadigitalarchive.org*>), a community-based online archive that documents, preserves and shares stories about South Asian American experiences in the United States.[2] The organisation seeks to counter the silences, under-representation and misrepresentation of South Asians in mainstream American archives and historical narratives through a publically accessible digital archive that reflects the community's century-old history in the US. The short records generated by the First Days Project represent a very brief window into this immigrant community which, taken as individual stories, personalises and complicates the metanarrative of immigration to the US and, taken collectively, reflects the diversity of South Asian immigrant experiences.

The records generated by First Days are not impartial by-products of activity as defined by the dominant Western archival tradition, but rather were created with the explicit goal of inclusion in an archives.[3] While more traditional archivists might deem this an 'artificial' collection, the First Days stories meet more pluralist definitions of records, such as that provided by Shannon Faulkhead, who writes: 'A record is any account, regardless of form, that preserves memory or knowledge of facts and events. A record can be a document, an individual's memory, an image, or a recording. It can also be an actual person, a community, or the land itself.'[4] As the stories generated by First Days preserve memory and knowledge of events, and they are included in a repository explicitly designed to make them accessible across space and time, the project is inherently archival in nature.

This paper defines and delineates the concept of participatory microhistory through an examination of SAADA's First Days Project. First, this paper will provide a brief overview of the history of SAADA and the First Days Project. Next, this paper will highlight three important functions filled by participatory microhistory projects like this one: the representation of groups not usually represented in the archive, the communication of affect and emotion as historically significant categories and the effective solicitation of community participation in the archival endeavour. Finally, this paper will expand on the concept of participatory microhistory as a tool to harness technology for community empowerment.

The primary method used for this paper is action research. Action research consists of 'critical reflection on experience of participating in action', and differs from case study method in the involvement of the researcher in the phenomenon he or she is investigating.[5] As Anne Gilliland and Sue McKemmish point out, this method has been used in archival studies in the collaborative development of archival projects between researchers and practitioners, as in Terry Cook's work on macroappraisal at the National Archives of Canada.[6] The first author of this paper is primarily a researcher (though also involved in archival activity) while the second author of this paper is primarily a practitioner (though also involved in research). In conducting this action research project, the authors of this paper hope to improve practice – not only their own practice as archivists for the South Asian American Digital Archive, but also the practice of others, as they hope this research inspires others to develop their own participatory microhistory projects. Through this research the authors also aim to reflect critically on the First Days Project, pointing out its successes as well as areas in need of improvement moving forward.

SAADA and the First Days Project

First, some brief background information on SAADA is necessary. SAADA is a US-based online community archival repository that the two authors co-founded in 2008. At that time, we were both working at the University of Chicago; Mallick was the Outreach Coordinator for the Center for Southern Asian Studies, Caswell was the Assistant Bibliographer for Southern Asia. We did an assessment of archival materials related to South Asian American history and found that no single repository was systematically collecting these materials and that none even had South Asian American history as a collecting priority. We sensed an urgent need; with much of the material history from the early twentieth century in the possession of children and grandchildren of first-generation immigrants who lack the capacity to preserve them, many of the South Asians who came after American immigration policy opened up in the Immigration & Nationality Act of 1965 aging, and many of the early community websites and born-digital materials from the 1990s disappearing, we felt that much of this history would be lost had someone not intervened. Furthermore, we sensed a real need for these materials to remain under community control and not be subsumed under larger institutional repositories, where they could be undervalued, get lost in the shuffle or misinterpreted. We also knew that we didn't have the financial resources or stability to create a physical space where the materials could be housed permanently.

So what do a librarian and community organiser do when faced with this dilemma? We pitched in $100 each, bought some server space, found a friend with experience managing non-profit finances to help us out, incorporated as a nongovernmental organisation and created the South Asian American Digital Archive as an independent, online-only, community-based repository. Five years later, SAADA holds the world's largest publicly accessible collection of materials documenting South Asian American experiences and remains the only non-profit organisation working nationally to document, preserve and provide access to the rich history of South Asians in the United States. We have a particular emphasis on collecting materials related to early South Asian immigration to the US, to anti-South Asian race riots, to labour, student and religious organisations, to political involvement, and to artists and intellectuals. We collect materials that are not just celebratory in nature, but reflect the diverse range of South Asian American experiences, from pamphlets created by Punjabi labourers organising against British rule in the 1910s to webzines created by Muslim punk bands in the 2010s. Through our collection priorities, we explicitly aim to counter the myth of South Asians as a model minority.[7] In this regard, we see ourselves not just as archivists, but anti-racist activists working towards a more inclusive society.

We define South Asian American as broadly as possible and take a transnational, regional approach. Our collection reflects records created by or about people residing in the United States who trace their heritage to Bangladesh, Bhutan, India, Maldives, Nepal, Pakistan, Sri Lanka and the many South Asian diaspora communities across the globe.[8] This later point – the many South Asian diaspora communities across the globe – is key to the inclusion of immigrants of South Asian descent from places like Trinidad and Fiji, where many Indians migrated as indentured labourers in the nineteenth century. Some of the descendants of these indentured labourers have migrated to the United States, forming substantial Indo-Caribbean communities (and to a lesser extent, Indo-Fijian communities) in places like Queens, New York. While these 'secondary diaspora' communities are often excluded from or overlooked by other South Asian American organisations, SAADA makes a concerted effort to include them in our collections.[9]

We are radically focused on access (in the sense that access is the primary archival service we provide) and still have no physical public location; we digitise historic materials and collect born-digital sources, archivally describe them using culturally appropriate terminology that the community itself uses, link them to related materials in the archives and make them freely accessible online to anyone in the world with an Internet connection. After digitisation, the physical materials remain with the individual, family, organisation or repository from which they originated. We currently have 1600 unique digital items in our collection and the archive is growing by the day.

SAADA is governed by a five-member board made up of two archivists, two professors whose work focuses on Asian American studies, and a non-profit development professional. Caswell is the only board member who is not of South Asian descent. We also have an amazing group of volunteers nationwide who help us track down, digitise and describe materials, as well as pro bono lawyers who helped us fill out the incorporation paperwork, craft our deed of gift and address copyright issues. Mallick is the organisation's only paid staff and we are in the middle of a fundraising campaign that aims to raise enough money to ensure his employment on a fulltime basis and hire additional staff. Fundraising is our biggest challenge, and, like many community organisations, we are trying to find the balance between independence and sustainability.[10] We use our website, online magazine, Facebook page, Twitter account and email list to update the public about our activities. SAADA board members have also presented at more than 40 events around the country, including numerous community forums across the US in which we solicit input on what our collection priorities should be and address any concerns or questions community members might have.

As an organisation run by professionally trained archivists, preservation is important to us, but we are also realistic and acknowledge that preservation is contingent. We digitise materials with the highest quality scanners using the Library of Congress's digitisation guidelines when possible, but we have also scanned materials using low-quality handheld scanners when individuals would not let their beloved grandfather's papers out of their homes. Adhering to the LOCKSS principle, we keep several back-up servers in cities across the US, as well as storing data in the cloud. We are committed to sound archival practice and the proper stewardship of digital materials into the future; we are also realists working with a limited budget and a volunteer staff. We had more than 153,000 unique visitors in 2013; this nearly triples the figure of 54,000 from the previous year. We are still working on ways to evaluate who uses SAADA and how, and how to gauge the level of engagement with the materials the collection and track our impact. Figuring out how best to measure our success is one of our biggest challenges, particularly given our pressing need to build ongoing relationships with funders.

Although SAADA is a unique organisation dealing with the particularities of one community's history, we have been inundated with requests from other community groups seeking advice on how to digitise and provide access to archival materials. It is clear from these requests that many community organisations are also seeking to take control of the means by which their own histories are documented, but many of these groups lack the infrastructure and expertise to harness the power of technology to increase community participation in archival collecting. SAADA hopes to serve as a model for these community groups.

In June 2013, SAADA launched its First Days Project. The project presents a departure from SAADA's previous efforts digitising pre-existing records in that it seeks to generate new audio, visual and textual records that record the experiences of South Asian immigrants about their first day in the United States. Community members generate many of these records themselves – either by recording their own narratives or interviewing others using video cameras, cellphones or personal computers. They then directly upload these files to SAADA; Mallick approves all files before they are made available to the public. The records that result are short in scope, limited to three minutes for audio and video, 300 words for text. SAADA's aim was to show the breadth of the South Asian American immigrant experience rather than explore any single narrative in depth. While this brevity limits what can be conveyed in each record, it also allows participants to condense their experiences into major themes and prevents them from being overwhelmed by pressure to create lengthy contributions. At the time of writing (December 2013), there are 89 stories included in the First Days Project.

Entries have reflected the national, regional and religious diversity of the community. First Days stories have ranged from a video interview with Basdeo Mangal, a Hindu priest who came from Guyana in 1996, to a textual narrative written by Rashna Batliwala Singh, who came from Mumbai to attend Mount Holyoke College in 1970, to a video narrative in American Sign Language recorded by Shaji Chacko, who came to the US from Hyderabad at age 11 in 1983.

Yet despite the diversity of these narratives, including narratives that reflect socio-economic diversity and diversity of immigration status has proved to be more of a struggle. Barriers of spare time and access to technology prevent many working-class immigrants from participating. This has been partially mitigated by SAADA volunteers conducting targeted interviews with working-class immigrants.[11] Furthermore, undocumented immigrants may not want to participate for fear that participation could attract unwanted attention from the Department of Homeland Security. We have offered participants the option of remaining anonymous, and indeed, the two anonymous entries we currently have are from recent immigrants from Pakistan who feel speaking candidly about their experiences may have a negative impact on their lives if attributed. Across all of the entries, we are keenly aware that participants are constructing narratives for public consumption and may leave out details that they wish to remain private.

Since its launch in June, the First Days Project section of the SAADA website has had nearly 18,000 unique page views (as of December 2013), representing nearly 10% of all total page views on the entire SAADA website in the same period. We've also observed that First Day stories are shared widely through social media and have heard anecdotally from a number of members of our user community about their excitement about the project.

First Days as digital participatory microhistory

While SAADA's First Days Project reflects the historical, social and cultural particularities of a specific community, the idea of using the Internet to generate short records directly from community members for inclusion in archives is not limited to this particular project or community. Indeed, we see First Days as a digital participatory microhistory project, which we define as any programmatic activity that uses Internet-based technologies to encourage community members to directly create short records for inclusion in an archives. Four elements are key to this definition: first, the project must use interactive digital technologies; second, it must facilitate the generation of new records directly by users themselves; third, these records must document some past or ongoing event or events, and finally, the records generated from such participation must be included in an archives where they are subject to archival interventions, such as preservation and description, and made publicly accessible. This definition builds on significant historiographical work on the concept of microhistory, updating participatory microhistory for the Internet age.[12] SAADA's status as a community archives also positions the First Days project as a community history project, defined by Thomson as 'history about a particular community, however defined, created in partnership with members of that community, and for the benefit of that community'.[13] Yet while SAADA is a community-based archives, participatory microhistory projects can be administered by institutions of all types, including government, university and corporate archives.[14]

Though the term 'digital participatory microhistory' is proposed by the authors of this paper, neither the type of project it describes, nor the underlying concepts, are unique to SAADA or to the First Days Project. Indeed, for the past decade archivists and scholars of archival studies have investigated ways in which Internet technologies can be used to increase user participation in the archival endeavour. A growing stream of archival scholarship has addressed the role of emerging Web 2.0 technologies in opening archival appraisal and description for user participation. Magia Krause and Elizabeth Yakel proposed harnessing digital platforms for participatory archival description.[15] Similarly, Huvila suggested archivists take advantage of digital technologies to encourage broader participation, experiment in decentralised curation and adopt a 'radical user orientation'.[16] In a rare overlap between the community archives and digital archives literature, Shilton and Srinivasan proposed to harness Web 2.0 technologies to encourage community participation in archival appraisal.[17] Yet, despite the theoretical importance of Shilton and Srinivasan's South Asia Web project and Krause and Yakel's Polar Bear Expedition 'second generation' finding aid, neither of these projects has involved user generation of records, nor have they proved to be sustainable in the long term.

By contrast, the Roy Rosenzweig Center for History and New Media at George Mason University has developed several web-based projects that fit the proposed definition of digital participatory microhistory. The Center's September 11 Digital Archive and its Hurricane Digital Memory Bank both allow users to directly upload text, audio, video and photographic files that document their experiences on or responses to major historical events.[18] The Center's Bracero History Archives also allows users to contribute a brief textual narrative about the migrant labourer program, which is then made publically available on the site.[19] Similarly, Moving Here, a project organised by the National Archives of the United Kingdom that involved 30 archives, libraries and museums from 2004 to 2007, created a platform whereby immigrants could directly contribute written narratives about their immigration experiences.[20] Although there are many other online projects that solicit user-generated content, very few of these projects have long-term preservation commitments.

Both SAADA's First Days Project and those of the Roy Rosenzweig Center for History and New Media take as precedent and are inspired by the ethos of oral history projects documenting twentieth-century American social movements. While many cultures have relied on oral transmission of information about the past for thousands of years, there was a distinct surge in interest in using oral history interviewing to document the lives of everyday people by American historians after World War II.[21] The popularity of oral history grew in the 1960s and 1970s, as historians like Howard Zinn and Studs Terkel called for greater academic attention to the historical importance of everyday people.[22] Participatory microhistories are logical extensions of these oral history projects in that they validate the historical importance of the lived experience of everyday people.

As creators of the First Days Project, we were also inspired by Helen Samuels' work on documentation strategy in the sense that we thought it was our duty as archivists to 'intervene in the records creation process' in order to document an under-documented community.[23] We agree wholeheartedly with Samuels' assertion that 'the concern is less what does exist than what should exist', and see First Days as a first step in envisioning what records should exist for the South Asian American community.[24] While inspired by both oral history projects and documentation strategy, we hope that participatory microhistory projects take the logic of such approaches a step further by encouraging everyday people to document their own experiences, eliminating (or at least diminishing the role of) intermediaries such as the historian taking the interview or the archivist appraising the record, and ensuring widespread access of such histories by everyday users through the Internet.[25]

What participatory microhistories do

Now that we have defined digital participatory microhistory and described some pre-cursors and examples, this article will now explicate their relevance. First, we argue that digital participatory microhistories can fill in gaps in the historic record by generating documentation of groups that are under-represented or misrepresented in archives. Secondly, by documenting the emotional aspects of historical events, participatory microhistories reveal the ways in which affect can be read as a historically significant category. And thirdly, participatory microhistories effectively get communities involved in archival collecting, breaking down barriers between archives and communities.

Participatory microhistories can be effective at generating records from groups whose histories are under-represented or misrepresented in archives. As anthropologist Michel-Rolph Trouillot describes, not all events are recorded and not all records make their way into archives.[26] Power dictates who has the ability, literacy level, time and means to create written records; women, the poor, and people of colour have, for many generations in the US, been unable, unlikely or less likely than dominant groups to create written records in the first place. Furthermore, when such records do exist, they have been undervalued and ignored by archivists, who have been and still are disproportionately drawn from positions of privilege.[27] Traditionally, archivists have neither actively gone out to recruit donors of materials from marginalised groups, nor have they emphasised the importance of such records in their appraisal decisions. The result is a horribly lopsided archival record that amplifies the voices of the powerful and further silences the marginalised.[28]

Participatory microhistory projects are one way that archivists can actively counter these silences. By soliciting records from marginalised groups and using Internet technologies to make such records widely accessible, archivists can ensure that at least some of these previously silenced voices will be heard.[29] While such projects are not a panacea that will cure all archival imbalances, they do fill important gaps where no previous material records existed or, when material records did exist, they would not have been deemed worthy of archivation.[30] In this way, participatory microhistory projects are concrete measures that archivists can take to give voice to marginalised groups.

The ability to give voice to those previously silent in the historic record was one of the prime motivating factors behind the First Days Project. As a community-based archive focused on collecting, preserving and sharing the records of South Asian Americans, we considered immigration and immigrant experiences to be top collecting priorities. Yet, the pre-existing material records surrounding immigration consist largely of bureaucratic documents like passports, visas and plane tickets. If we were going to rely solely on these administrative records to tell the stories of South Asian immigrants to the US, what stories would we be telling and what would we be missing? Whose voices would we be privileging? At whose expense?

Bureaucratic records are created by bureaucrats; they do not (at least not straightforwardly) reflect the voices of the subjects whose lives they seek to administer.[31] Soliciting participatory microhistories fills in this gap by generating records that give voice in the archives to those who have no voice in the pre-existing historical record.

In this way, it constitutes a form of archival activism in which archivists can generate records to counter silences rife in the historical record.

Here, let us provide just a few examples of First Days stories that capture voices that would otherwise go unheard. CM Naim came to San Francisco from Kolkata, India in 1957 at age 21. Naim's luggage – which contained his passport, his degrees, 25 US dollars (his only American money) and directions on how to get to the International House at the University of California, Berkeley, where Naim would stay – was lost at the airport. Alone, confused and exhausted, Naim sat down and started crying. A stranger offered to help, tracked down the woman who had accidentally taken Naim's bag and convinced a cab driver to take Naim to retrieve the bag. After retrieving the bag, Naim narrates:

> I then asked him [the cab driver] if he could take me straight to the International House in Berkeley. It was on the other side of the Bay, and there were tolls to pay. I showed him the money I had. 'Was it enough?' He nodded, and away we went. Gradually, my senses crept back into me. I began to see the sights, hear the noises, feel the air blowing in. And then suddenly a whole new sense of confidence filled me.
>
> There we were, on that amazing bridge, with vast stretches of sun-lit blue water spread underneath us. A powerful machine was speeding me ever so smoothly to a destination that now seemed so certain. The cab no doubt had a roof, but it felt as if there was no barrier of any kind between this world and me. An openness prevailed. The new world held no terror for me any more. I had witnessed a miracle, wrought by a total stranger who had helped me when I had no one to turn to and lost all hope. I gained that day a kind of confidence and feeling of trust that has come to my rescue many a time since then. Not that I have not despaired since that day. I've hit the bottom several times. I have been lonely and angry and terrified, and worse. I have experienced exploitation and racial prejudice. But thanks to that day I have always managed not to blame some anonymous America for my troubles.[32]

In this brief narrative, Naim eloquently communicates the highs and lows of being an immigrant, and provides a perspective on South Asian American immigrant experiences that are not commonly found in archives. His is not a story that could be effectively communicated through administrative records. Naim's first day is much more than his passport, more than his boarding pass, more than the directions he carried. Without Naim telling the story in his own words, we (and future users of archives) would miss the context that might make those administrative records worthy of archiving. We would miss the detail that can only come from a first-person account. We would also miss an essential component of immigrant experiences, the despair and the redemption that are often two sides of the same coin. Without the First Days Project, Naim's story would likely never be included in an archives.

Similarly, without First Days, the story of Bernard Despot, an immigrant of Indian descent who came from Port of Spain, Trinidad to Queens, New York in 1989, would likely never wind up in an archives. In his three-minute video narrative, he recounts:

> My name is Bernard Despot and I am 60 years old. I am also a citizen of the United States and I have to say that this did not come easy. I came here in the year 1989. I was about 38 years old. I worked very very hard for everything that I have but the United States has given me that opportunity. I am a resident of Queens [New York] where I have lived since the time I first came here … I achieved a lot. I have seen my three children go through college. I myself, have taken the opportunity to get my GED [high school diploma equivalency] … It is all a challenging process. It is very tough. I have worked many places, as a

> dishwasher …, as a parking attendant, I have driven buses for Greyhound, and finally I am working as a shuttle driver for the Hilton Hotel. I have worked a lot of places to achieve the things that I want. The successes that I have came with very, very hard work.
>
> I remember when I first came to this country, one of the first things I remember and I will always remember is the street vendors. I remember the souvlaki and the gyros, it was around Christmas time, and I can get the smell of that food in my nose. And even now, every time it's Christmas, I get that smell, and it brings me right back to my first time in the United States …[33]

For Despot, being an immigrant has meant hard work, sacrifice and watching his children succeed in ways he could not, but it has also meant encountering the strange smell of other immigrants' foods. This visceral detail, especially when contextualised within Despot's narrative of hard work, conveys important historical information about what it feels like to start a new life far away from home.

Yet, like Naim's story, Despot's would not likely be deemed worthy of archiving by most mainstream repositories. Despot is, after all, a working-class immigrant of colour who did not directly play a role in any major historical event. While each short individual account may not seem historically significant, taken together they are 'evidence of us' to use Sue McKemmish's apt phrase, conveying crucial information about what it was like to be a South Asian American immigrant.[34] Without SAADA, this evidence of us would go uncollected.

Furthermore, as Naim's and Despot's stories confirm, the participatory microhistories generated by the First Days Project reveal the importance of affect in ways that administrative records do not. For the immigrants whose stories are recorded through the First Days Project, their experiences leaving home, travelling halfway around the world and building a new life in a strange country are much more than their visa stamps; they are narratives animated by sorrow, joy, pride, excitement and confusion.

Loneliness is a common thread in the First Days Project. Participant Ali Khataw arrived in Fayetteville, Arkansas from Karachi, Pakistan in 1980. In his audio interview with Mallick, he said:

> But the first day when I arrived it was... I don't know what to say... it was... very lonely. You don't have the people that you have been growing up with. Your friends, your parents, your sister, brother. And then you come over and then suddenly it's a different environment and you don't have a single friend. I mean zero. Zilch. You're starting with a blank slate. And I create friends very easily and all that, but loneliness was the number one... if you want me to put it in one word... initially the first day was loneliness because you don't have anybody to count on, you don't know who to ask for advice and you don't know if they're going to give you the right advice. It was very interesting. It was different. I think helpless and loneliness were the two words that I would put the experience into the first day. Now... ask me about after a month? Oh my god, I was a party animal![35]

Khataw's interview is accompanied by a snapshot of him in a dorm room, looking every bit the party animal part.

Loneliness was also a key theme of Tahrat Naushaba Shahid's written entry. Shahid travelled from Dhaka, Bangladesh to South Hadley, Massachusetts in 1997 to attend college. She wrote:

> My first night, once I got there and we'd dropped off my things and I got out my bedsheets and I was settled in, it was pitch-dark outside the window and completely quiet.

> I kind of understood the term 'thundering silence' for the first time. 'Cause, where I grew up, I used to hear rickshaws ting-tinging outside and prostitutes fighting and things, you know? And now, nothing. Just quiet! I think I cried that first night [laughs] – I'm pretty sure I cried, like, all night that night. It was pretty scary. It was, oddly, the loneliest I've ever felt because, having grown up in such a big, busy city, and I was 17. So, that was the first culture-shock moment.[36]

Shahid's entry is accompanied by her initial US visa bearing a 'Cancelled without Prejudice' stamp. The official government record serves as a visual to supplement and corroborate the text, but it is clear the important record is the narrative.

All four of the First Day stories highlighted here are animated by emotion. Naim's despair and elation, Despot's pride, and Khataw's and Shahid's loneliness each convey essential elements of immigrant experiences that would go undocumented if we were to rely solely on official records.[37] The emotional encounters with the archive enabled by participatory microhistories connect people to the past in ways that administrative records cannot. A classroom full of college first years cares little about a cancelled visa, but a videotaped narrative that invokes pride, sacrifice and the smell of gyros brings history to life; immigrants are no longer faceless masses, but become real people with hopes and fears to whom students can relate. In this way, emotion becomes a teaching tool, a way into the archive for new groups of users. Furthermore, even scholarly users of archives have expressed increasing interest in the historical significance of emotion over the past three decades. For scholars influenced by 'the affective turn' such as Eve Kosofsky Sedwick and Sara Ahmed, emotions are not just archival entry points, but a primary object of study.[38] Enabled by participatory microhistories, the expression of emotions conveys powerful information about the past not commonly found in official records.

Finally, participatory microhistory projects enable archives to effectively solicit community participation in the archival endeavour. Before SAADA launched the First Days Project, we actively solicited archival materials from South Asian American communities through in-person forums across the country. We also solicit materials through a prominent 'contribute' button on our website, which outlines our collection development policy and provides an email address where potential donors of materials can contact us. We have also been very successful at getting community members involved through SAADA's Facebook page, through which we have solicited translations of materials in South Asian languages, contextual information about photographic records and questions to ask the subjects of oral history interviews. In addition to the success of these outreach efforts, the First Days Project has generated unprecedented community interest. Not only has the project generated more than 80 entries thus far, it has moreover proven to be an effective way to engage SAADA's existing user community and engage new constituents. During a recent visit to Austin, Texas for the grand opening of the Asian American Resource Center, Mallick recorded nearly 15 first-day stories from local community members. These are 15 new people who are now invested in SAADA's mission.

First Days has also generated a great deal of interest from the media. On 29 August 2013, the project was featured on Public Radio International's show 'The World', and listeners were encouraged to call in to share their own stories.[39] 'You could easily miss American stories like these if nobody was around to collect them', the story concluded.[40] The same story was later rebroadcast on the BBC World Service program 'Boston Calling'. Five major Indian American publications – *India West*, *Desi Talk*,

IndoAmerican News, *News India Times* and *India Abroad* – ran features on the project, as did four newspapers in India, including *The Times of India*.[41] While the SAADA board originally intended First Days to be a limited, six-week project, the overwhelming response we have gotten from the community and the press has led us to continue the project indefinitely.

As SAADA's experience has shown, participatory microhistory projects demonstrate how archives value the everyday experiences of community members, and in turn, get community members to value the archives. In this way, participatory microhistories forge symbiotic bonds that are crucial to other aspects of archival practice such as collecting records, promoting use and fundraising. A community member who feels his or her story has a place in the archives is more likely to donate physical materials, tell other community members to use the archives and make a monetary gift. These symbiotic bonds are especially important for community-based archives trying to represent diverse voices, as such projects can be designed to target groups who are, at present, under-represented in the archives. Furthermore, participatory microhistory projects effectively convey that archives are about sharing stories. When we try to explain to community members that archives collect records and records are evidence of activity, their eyes glaze over, they get despondent and they change the subject. When we explain to community members that archives are about sharing stories with people in the present to increase understanding in the future, they get excited, they become engaged and they understand the importance of archival work.

Conclusion: Using technology for community participation

As we have discussed in this article, digital participatory microhistory projects harness the power of the Internet to solicit and distribute short records of archival significance. These projects can successfully contribute to archives by filling in historical gaps, by documenting emotion and affect, and by directly involving community members in the archival endeavour.

Above all, digital participatory microhistory projects reveal how widespread technologies such as the Internet, word-processing software and built-in recording devices can be used to enrich archives and, in turn, empower the communities whose histories they seek to document and preserve. While digital divides still present significant challenges (particularly to representing poor and working-class people), commonplace technologies can be liberatory tools for archival activism, if only archives actively engage them.

Over the past few decades, archives have been plagued by problems: historic and current imbalances in power and representation in the records we collect, increasing pressure to digitise records despite decreasing fiscal support and widespread disinterest in, mistrust of and/or misunderstanding of archives. In response, archivists have done an inadequate job demonstrating our value to society. While digital participatory microhistory projects will not entirely solve these significant challenges, they do represent a small way to get communities to care about archives. And caring, we hope, is the first step in building strong relationships that can ensure that archives remain meaningful institutions in the future.

Notes

1. SAADA, 'First Days: FAQ', available at *<http://www.saadigitalarchive.org/firstdays/faq>*, accessed 22 October 2013.
2. SAADA defines South Asia very broadly; the collection reflects the vast range of experiences of those in the United States who trace their heritage to Bangladesh, Bhutan, India, Maldives, Nepal, Pakistan, Sri Lanka and the many South Asian diaspora communities across the globe.
3. For a discussion of impartiality rooted in the dominant Western archival tradition, see Terry Eastwood, 'What is Archival Theory and Why is it Important?' *Archivaria*, no. 37, Spring 1994, pp. 122–130.
4. Shannon Faulkhead, 'Connecting Through Records: Narratives of Koorie Victoria', *Archives & Manuscripts*, vol. 37, no. 2, p. 67.
5. A Gilliland and S McKemmish, 'Building an Infrastructure for Archival Research', *Archival Science*, vol. 4, nos 3–4, 2004, p. 184.
6. Ibid. For an example, see T Cook, 'Appraisal Methodology: Macro-Appraisal and Functional Analysis. Part A: Concepts and Theory' and 'Part B: Guidelines for Performing an Archival Appraisal on Government Records', 2002, available at *<http://www.collectionscanada.gc.ca/government/disposition/007007-1035-e.html>*, accessed 22 October 2013.
7. The American Immigration and Nationality Act of 1965 gave preference to highly educated immigrants, resulting in a 'brain drain' from South Asia to the US, and the common American stereotyping of Indians as quiet, hard-working, apolitical professionals. For more information see Vijay Prashad, *The Karma of Brown Folk*, University of Minnesota Press, Minneapolis, 2000.
8. 'South Asia' emerged as a term during the Cold War and reflects the interests of US military intelligence in the region. It is by no means meant to convey political coherence; many of the nation-states included under the rubric of South Asia have since engaged in armed conflict. While many first-generation immigrants from the region are more likely to identify along nationalist, religious, linguistic or regional lines, the second generation is likely to identify as South Asian American. For more information on the complicated issue of identity among South Asian Americans, and the role archives like SAADA play in identity formation, see Michelle Caswell, 'Inventing New Archival Imaginaries: Theoretical Foundations for Identity-Based Community Archives', in D Daniel and A S Levi (eds), *Identity Palimpsests: Archiving Ethnicity in the U. S. and Canada*, Litwin Books, Los Angeles, 2014, forthcoming.
9. For more information on Indians in Trinidad, see Viranjini Munasinghe, *Callaloo or Tossed Salad? East Indians and the Cultural Politics of Identity in Trinidad,* Cornell University Press, Ithaca, NY, 2001.
10. A Flinn, M Stevens and E Shepherd, 'Whose Memories, Whose Archives? Independent Community Archives, Autonomy, and the Mainstream', *Archival Science*, vol. 9, nos 1–2, 2009, pp. 71–86.
11. Kamal Badhey's interview with Basdeo Mangal is a good example of this. SAADA, 'First Days: Basdeo Mangal', available at *<http://www.saadigitalarchive.org/firstdays/story/3019>*, accessed 22 October 2013.
12. The term 'microhistory' has been used by historians for at least the past 40 years. See Carlo Ginzburg, 'Microhistory: Two or Three Things That I Know About it', in *Threads and Traces*: *True False Fictive*, University of California Press, Berkeley, 2012, pp. 193–214.
13. Alistair Thomson, 'Oral History and Community History in Britain: Personal and Critical Reflections on Twenty-Five Years of Continuity and Change', *Oral History*, vol. 36, no. 1, 2008, p. 97.
14. While definitions of community are contextual and shifting, Flinn, Stevens and Shepherd define community as 'any manner of people who come together and present themselves as such, and a "community archive" is the product of their attempts to document the history of their commonality' (p. 75).
15. M Krause and E Yakel, 'Interaction in Virtual Archives: The Polar Bear Expedition Digital Collections Next Generation Finding Aid', *American Archivist*, vol. 70, no. 2, 2007, pp. 282–314.

16. I Huvila, 'Participatory Archive: Towards Decentralised Curation, Radical User Orientation, and Broader Conextualisation of Records Management', *Archival Science*, vol. 8, no. 1, 2008, pp. 15–36.
17. K Shilton and R Srinivasan, 'Participatory Appraisal and Arrangement for Multicultural Archival Collections', *Archivaria*, no. 63, Spring 2007, pp. 87–101.
18. Roy Rosenzweig Center for History and New Media at George Mason University, '911 Digital Archive', available at *<http://911digitalarchive.org>*, accessed 22 October 2013. Roy Rosenzweig Center for History and New Media at George Mason University, 'Hurricane Archive', available at *<http://www.hurricanearchive.org>*, accessed 22 October 2013.
19. Roy Rosenzweig Center for History and New Media at George Mason University, 'Bracero Archive', available at *<http://braceroarchive.org>*, accessed 22 October 2013.
20. National Archives of the United Kingdom, 'Moving Here', available at <http://www.moving-here.org.uk>, accessed 17 December 2013.
21. A more detailed history of the oral history movement is beyond the scope of this paper. See Donald A Ritchie, *Doing Oral History*, Oxford University Press, New York, 2003, pp. 19–46.
22. H Zinn, 'Secrecy, Archives and the Public Interest', *The Midwestern Archivist*, vol. 2, no. 2, 1977, pp. 14–26. Studs Terkel, *Working*, Pantheon, New York, 1972.
23. HW Samuels, 'Who Controls the Past', *American Archivist*, vol. 49, no. 2, Spring 1986, p. 122.
24. Ibid., p. 120.
25. We do not mean to imply that the archivist has no role in participatory microhistory projects, but rather this role shifts from appraiser to conceiver of the project, designer of the system that enables the project and allows access to it, and promoter and advocate of the project.
26. Michel-Rolph Trouillot, *Silencing the Past: Power and the Production of History*, Beacon, Boston, 1995.
27. Zinn, pp. 14–26. A recent survey conducted by the Society of American Archivists revealed that 89% of archivists in the US self-identify as white. Society of American Archivists, 'Membership Needs & Satisfaction Survey', available at <http://files.archivists.org/membership/surveys/saaMemberSurvey-2012r2.pdf>, accessed 13 December 2013.
28. Ibid., RS Carter, 'Of Things Said and Unsaid: Power, Archival Silences, and the Power in Silence', *Archivaria*, no. 61, Spring 2006, pp. 215–233.
29. Thomson, pp. 95–104.
30. By 'archivation', I mean deemed worthy of inclusion in an archives. V Harris, 'Genres of the Trace: Memory, Archives and Trouble', *Archives and Manuscripts*, vol. 40, no. 3, 2012, pp. 147–157.
31. There has been much discussion of late about reading against the grain of bureaucratic records to uncover the voices of the enslaved, colonised or otherwise marginalised. See J Bastian, 'Reading Colonial Records Through an Archival Lens: The Provenance of Place, Space, and Creation', *Archival Science*, vol. 6, nos 3–4, 2006, pp. 267–284. See also C Hurley, 'Parallel Provenance: What if Anything is Archival Description?' *Archives and Manuscripts*, vol. 33, no. 1, 2005, pp. 110–145.
32. SAADA, 'First Days: C.M. Naim', available at *<http://www.saadigitalarchive.org/firstdays/story/3187>*, accessed 22 October 2013.
33. SAADA, 'First Days: Bernard Despot', available at <http://www.saadigitalarchive.org/firstdays/story/3182>, accessed 22 October 2013.
34. S McKemmish, 'Evidence of Me', *Archives and Manuscripts*, vol. 24, no. 1, May 1996, pp. 28–45. See also S McKemmish, 'Evidence of Me... in a Digital World', in *I, Digital: Personal Collections in the Digital Era*, Christopher A Lee (ed.), Society of American Archivists, Chicago, 2011, pp. 115–148.
35. SAADA, 'First Days: Ali Khataw', available at *<http://www.saadigitalarchive.org/firstdays/story/2854>*, accessed 22 October 2013.
36. SAADA, 'First Days: Tahrat Naushaba Shahid', available at *<http://www.saadigitalarchive.org/firstdays/story/3063>*, accessed 22 October 2013.
37. While such vivid descriptions of emotion might have been written down in letters sent back home, it is unlikely that such letters would wind up in archives, particularly in archives in the US.

38. See Eve Kosofsky Sedwick, *Touching Feeling: Affect, Pedagogy, Performativity,* Duke University Press, Durham, NC, 2003 and Sara Ahmed, *The Cultural Politics of Emotion*, Routledge, New York, 2004. For a broader sweep, see Melissa Gregg and Gregory J Seigworth (eds), *The Affect Theory Reader*, Duke University Press, Durham, NC, 2010.
39. The World, 'First Days: South Asian Americans Share Their Stories of Arrival in America', available at *<http://www.theworld.org/2013/08/first-days-south-asian-americans-share-stories-of-their-first-days-in-america/>*, accessed 22 October 2013.
40. Ibid.
41. For a full listing of press coverage, visit SAADA, 'Press', available at *<http://www.saadigitalarchive.org/press>*, accessed 22 October 2013.

Archiving the wild, the wild archivist: Bukit Brown Cemetery and Singapore's emerging 'docu-tivists'

Natalie Pang and Liew Kai Khiun

Natalie Pang is an Assistant Professor at the Wee Kim Wee School of Communication and Information at Nanyang Technological University, Singapore. She acquired her doctorate from Monash University, Australia, where her thesis involving the study of participatory design and common pool resources in cultural institutions received two awards. Her current programme of research involves participatory archives and engagement in cultural institutions, and the relationship between message design and information-seeking behaviour in participatory contexts.

Liew Kai Khiun has been involved in conservation issues in Singapore for more than a decade and is also engaged in scholarly research on the relationship between new media and conservation in Singapore. He obtained his BA (hons) and MA at the National University of Singapore and was awarded his doctorate from University College London. Kai Khiun is currently an Assistant Professor at the Wee Kim Wee School of Communication and Information at Nanyang Technological University, Singapore.

In recent years there has been growing interest in the discipline of computing in relation to cultural heritage, parallel with developments in greater user participation in archives and advances in documentation work. These trends are reflected in the case of a documentation project of an old Chinese cemetery in Singapore, Bukit Brown Cemetery. This case was characterised by tensions among the 'wild' array of emerging individual participants and archivists that took the momentum away from both more formal NGOs and government institutions in documenting, archiving and raising awareness of the heritage of the site when part of it was announced to be set aside for a new highway. The case presents a compelling need for participatory archives, facilitated by computing interventions encouraging public engagement and visits to the site. Being actively involved in the documentation process, the authors reflect on how conceptual frameworks of records may assist in designing new media innovations and informing the ways by which a cemetery may be documented. Through these reflections, the authors argue for the active participation of archivists and records professionals in documentation work, and demonstrate how, in the creation and keeping of records, they shape the collective imagination of the public and other stakeholders in heritage sites.

Introduction

Not long after my dad passed away in 2011, the government announced plans for an 8 lane highway that would cut through Bukit Brown, and graves in the way would have to be exhumed. The news of the highway triggered a memory. The last time I visited my grand-

> pa's tomb was more than 40 years ago when I was a young girl. I could vividly recall my grandpa's tomb at Bukit Brown. Concerned it might be affected, I realised it was time to visit him … Inscribed on the tombstone was my ancestral hometown, Kimen, my grandfather's death date, 1937, and the names of his children. My father was the only son. For the first time I came to know my father's birth name 陈天吉, Tan Tien Kiat, inscribed on the tomb. My grandpa passed away when my dad was only five and dad changed to a simpler name, 陈 亞 旺, Tan Ah Ong. (Serene Tan, 'My Father's Dream Fulfilled', 4 February 2012)[1]

This is one of the numerous entries on the website *All Things Bukit Brown: Heritage, Habitat and History*, which was set up by a community of concerned members of the Singaporean public known as the Brownies. The purpose of the website has been to raise awareness of both the ecological and heritage value of the Chinese cemetery comprising an estimated 100,000 graves, now hidden within the lush equatorial vegetation that has covered the site since burials ceased in 1973. Established in 1923, the 173 acres of Bukit Brown Cemetery (BBC) came to the forefront of cultural politics in 2011 when the Singaporean government announced that part of it would have to give way for a highway, and the other parts for the development of residences in the longer term. In a country where cemeteries have been regularly cleared since the end of the colonial era for urban developments, the public outcry following the announcement may have been surprising to the government. In response, the government commissioned a documentation team of academics, including the two authors of the present article, to document the graves in the area affected by the planned eight-lane highway project, and create an archive that would be of public interest and useful for future scholarly research. Some members of the documentation team, including the second author of this paper, actively participate and interact with the Brownies behind the website *All Things Bukit Brown*. Some of the Brownies also volunteer for the documentation team. The work of the documentation team is independent of the activities and interests of the Brownies.

The community of Brownies had been exceptionally active in their efforts to keep BBC relevant to the broader public. They have helped descendants to find gravestones, brought in guided tours and tracked the material cultures of the tomb designs. In addition, they have traced the genealogies and histories of the deceased, exploring the broader contexts of the lives of those buried in the cemetery, ranging from prominent business leaders to revolutionaries. It is through the efforts of these Brownies that the cemetery was placed under the World Monuments Fund Watchlist in 2014, a list that documents endangered heritage sites from around the world.[2]

The graphic illustration in Figure 1 by Cartoon Press, an independent anonymous cartoonist known for his critique of the Singaporean government through his posts on Facebook, typifies the activities of the Brownies. Carrying out a range of activities entailing research, public education and advocacy, this loose association of individuals has been trying to keep the future of BBC in the public limelight. Through public tours conducted by spirited volunteers every weekend, which have led an estimated 10,000 people through the cemetery since the issue surfaced, the Brownies have been trying to keep a human presence in this otherwise neglected space in order to dispel notions that it is redundant land awaiting infrastructural redevelopment by the state. In addition, they have also pre-empted the official documentation team by launching public exhibitions and lectures on BBC at various venues. Similarly, with related websites, blogs and social media accounts, including the main Singapore Heritage–Bukit Brown Cemetery

Figure 1. Cartoon Press, 'The Great Bukit Brownies', posted on 19 November 2013. Reproduced with permission.

Facebook page, the Brownies have worked hard to keep their online presence visible and active.

Wright foresaw the possibility of such heritage sites producing public memories through acts of visitation, rediscovery and re-knowing through engagement with the material archives by successive generations.[3] In the case of BBC, the Brownies through their engagement with the material documents of the site and interactions with the documentation team have also become amateur or 'wild archivists'. Through their personal research and involvement, they have created a rich repository of information and knowledge about BBC as well as the broader historical context in which the deceased had lived. Here, the digital cultures of the Internet and social media have facilitated in sourcing, collecting, processing and sharing significant records accompanied by meaningful reflections in cyberspace. The reflections of Serene Tan quoted at the start of this article in some ways represent a more active form of participation in one of the many un-orchestrated individual efforts aiming to rescue the repository of genealogical and historical materials that are contained within these graves.

Wright's attempts to reveal the apparent trade-offs between housing the living against that of the dead underscores a developmentalist and functionalist mindset that typified the trends of a modern governance that is less restrained by the religious–cultural taboos of traditional societies as understood by Giddens.[4] The ideas of extensional and intensional transformations to be expected in modern societies were presented by Giddens in his 1991 book *The Consequences of Modernity*. Giddens reflected on the complexity, characteristics, changes and transformations one should expect of contemporary societies. Modernity in the context of this paper refers to the influences that Europe exerted upon colonial societies from the seventeenth century onwards, distinguished by the rise of capitalism, industrial revolution, rationality and orientation towards progress. Giddens argues that modernity has brought about complex modes of being or existence. On the one hand, there are what Giddens calls extensional transformations, such as the invention of the printing press and the introduction of participatory media, which are those related to a person or organisation that has global connections and is no longer only confined to the local. These social connections in turn result in assumptions and expectations as to how one should function, exist and behave as part of existing in this world. This existence is mediated by intensional factors: one's intimate desires, goals and reflections.

In the case of BBC, globalising influences driving the urgency for urban development, and likewise the availability of information and communication technologies in enabling and making dialogical communication possible, present extensional transformations. On the other hand, the everyday practices of individuals, even as they make choices concerning their engagement with the significance and issue of BBC, make up intensional transformations. Currently, enthusiastic individuals and civil society groups are already being transformed intensionally using social media tools such as Facebook and blogs[5] (see Figure 2 for an example).

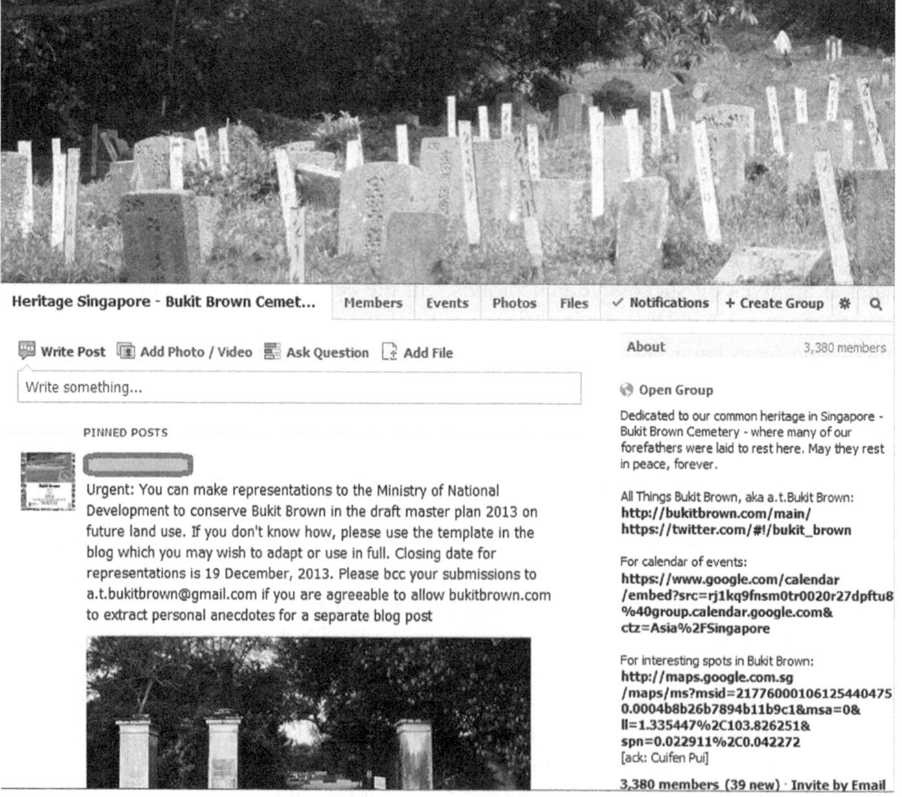

Figure 2. An example of a Facebook group to facilitate engagement: a type of intensional transformation.

At these sites, interested users are allowed to freely post their reflections after visiting the site, pursue active causes (such as the one posted here) and participate in the construction of collective wisdom about records and historical information related to each grave. Since the establishment of Facebook groups and websites for BBC, the significance of the cemetery has gained steady momentum – among academics, the Singapore Heritage Society, the National Heritage Board of Singapore, civil society groups, the government, citizens and, now, the international community with the entry of BBC on the World Monuments Fund's Watchlist.[6] Arguably, without social media the value and meaning of BBC to Singaporean society may never have been so explored or constructed.

Documentation and technology

Since 2011 the authors have been involved as part of a working team to participate in and coordinate the documentation of graves that are potentially affected by the construction of the highway – estimated to be around 3746 graves out of more than 100,000 in the 213-acre site.[7] Through locating, identifying, copying, translating and coding the affected graves with the deployment of a range of photo-videographic technologies, including the use of drones to capture the layout of the larger monuments belonging to more prominent historical personalities, one aspect of the documentation effort focuses on the material aspects of the cemetery as a physical site. Video recordings of exhumations and rituals, oral history interviews with caretakers of the site and descendants of those buried in BBC comprise the immaterial component of the documentation project. This latter could lead to further archival research into the social histories and memories associated with the cemetery site, but also the broader sociocultural significance of the legacy of the Chinese diaspora in Singapore.

The authors have been assisting the principal project director, Dr Hui Yew Foong, by connecting him with computing engineers, designers and photo-ethnographers to use the latest applications in digital and information technologies to layer and network the physical site with a proof-of-concept augmented reality system.[8] Apart from designing signage and directional maps, these professionals have worked, on a voluntary basis, to design interactive and non-invasive software, especially mobile phone apps, to allow users to retrieve relevant curated archival digitised materials instantaneously while visiting the cemetery site. The documentation team has also been working with the National Library Board of Singapore with the goal of accessioning the eventual archive for public access. With more knowledge acquired about BBC as a result of the participatory archive, the documentation team has been able to pursue missions of outreach and advocacy. For instance, public debates on the heritage value of BBC have been conducted with schools.

Having a rather lean documentation team meant heavy reliance on volunteers to help complete the necessary work. With hindsight their involvement had a positive impact on the perceptions of BBC's cultural and heritage value, creating a pool of engaged citizens who were always more than willing to offer their knowledge, time and resources to the work of the BBC documentation project. The volunteers also helped to champion and actively promote the BBC project to fellow Singaporeans as well as the international community, thereby altering the ways by which stakeholders, including archivists, engage in interdisciplinary dialogues about a heritage site. The shift of power towards citizens who are potential users of the eventual archive, underlined by principles of equality and rationality, permeates these dialogues. Without a doubt, there is much historical and cultural value in BBC, but to us, the BBC site is important because its very existence and process of engagement reflect the collective aspirations of stakeholders.

Passionate engagement is usually accompanied by advocacy. The documentation project took place concurrently with a more heated ongoing public debate over the future of BBC that put the government's plans under a more critical spotlight. Apart from the open reservations to the plans expressed by formal non-governmental organisations such as the Singapore Heritage Society and the Nature Society of Singapore, there was also a growing group of activists who were simultaneously volunteering in the documentation project and part of the Brownies as well. This group has an explicit and focused goal in wanting to preserve BBC as a heritage park.

As activists and volunteers to document BBC, or what we will term 'docu-tivists', this emerging group have actively contributed their own narratives to various aspects of BBC, such as the discoveries of unattended graves and connections to historical and sociocultural contexts. In the process they have become self-taught domain experts and providers of knowledge to interested members of the public, and have spearheaded new forms of advocacy and civil society in Singapore.

The tension arising from the need to preserve the heritage and cultural value of BBC while confronted with growing urbanisation and developmental needs presents a compelling case for technological interventions. Firstly, there is much urgency to document information about the site, and specifically the cultural aspects of BBC, within an interactive system that can facilitate users' engagement with the heritage site. Secondly, an interactive system would also provide an opportunity for individuals to engage with the information and cultural aspects documented, as well as with each other. In a direct way, the system will also facilitate intensional transformations as both Brownies and visitors reflect on the content and make choices with regards to heritage engagement and appraising records as they are being created.

Archiving in the 'wild': opportunities and challenges

As highlighted by Huvila,[9] compared to other memory institutions such as libraries and museums, archives in places such as Singapore have not always been as inclined to involve users or undertake evaluation studies with users. In Huvila's view, this was because archives have always held that users who come to the archives know what they want, the presumption being that they are largely historians and researchers who approach archives seeking particular data and records for their work. In addition to this argument, from our observations over the years it may be due to the administrative boundaries between the work of libraries, museums and archives. In doing so, it creates disciplinary differences between memory institutions and the professional work conducted within each institution. For users, however, such differences are almost invisible. In the case of a heritage site such as Bukit Brown Cemetery, the user is interested in seeking information, engaging in multi-sensory experiences via visual, written and auditory records, and would like to see all of what they themselves perceive as being important included in an archive for long-term storage and preservation.

Because of the pressing need to capture the full tangible and intangible value of the site, the documentation project was composed of people from diverse backgrounds: historians, archivists, photographers, sociologists and computer engineers. This provided archivists with opportunities to build in functionalities and tasks that could enhance knowledge about Bukit Brown Cemetery via contributions from the community. For instance, the computer engineers that were developing the augmented reality application provided feedback that led to the development of functionalities that would allow users to contribute their own knowledge on various artefacts within the site. Additionally, the historians, sociologists and anthropologists on the team emphasised the importance of in-depth knowledge and the way they created meanings and made sense of the materials, which provided insight into how users may eventually engage with the evolving archive of Bukit Brown Cemetery.

The technologies in use (the Facebook page, the augmented reality application), and the documentation and archiving work, function as systemic agents in facilitating both extensional and intensional transformations. The Facebook page and augmented reality application make international connectivity and interactions possible, and prompt extensional transformations with increased velocity. As interactive systems for individuals, these technological interventions facilitate intensional transformations as individuals use such systems to interact with information and cultural artefacts at the BBC site. Users need not visit the site in order to participate, but we have observed that these systems heighten curiosity about the site and ultimately transform virtual visitors into visiting the physical site. At the same time this provides opportunities for users to participate in the creation of what will eventually become a long-term archive. This archive should include records about the cemetery and records of participation; with the latter representing evidence of how members of a society, through their interests, shape knowledge about their own heritage and collective identity. This latter category of records is perhaps even more important than the first group of records, as they function as records of how a particular society makes sense of its own heritage and collective identity. But both types of records should work together to reflect the conversational tone and context by which historical knowledge about various aspects of the cemetery is constructed.

The example shown in Figure 3, for instance, shows how members of a community consisting of both experts and general visitors may interact with each other and construct important records about various aspects of the cemetery, in this case, tiles used at selected graves.

The documentation team, recognising the importance of records being created in the digital spaces of Facebook and smartphone augmented reality applications, has been capturing and keeping records since 2012 for appraisal at a later time. The immediate work ahead has to do with deciding how such records should be appraised, and by whom. Duranti has described appraisal as the 'process of establishing the value of documents made or received … qualifying that value, and determining its duration'.[10] In the same paper, Duranti explores how value is attributed, but suggests that there has been little discussion as to who should be allocating and establishing such values. This is not for reasons of neglect: traditionally, the process of creating and governing archives has always been typically left to the archivists.

To be truly participative, users should also be empowered to participate in the appraisal and selection of records, a project we have already begun planning within the Bukit Brown Cemetery documentation team. But given the size and diversity of users, the task is at best daunting, and at its worst chaotic and costly. Yet the benefits arguably outweigh the costs, since the process of appraisal and selection is itself perhaps one of the best ways to help archives and users understand each other, for archivists and other stakeholders think differently about how best to arrange and describe the records, and promote long-term usage to justify the sustainability of the archive. The role of archivists in a participatory archive is thus one with an expanded set of competencies. The need to go beyond basic understandings of archival theory and document sensibilities

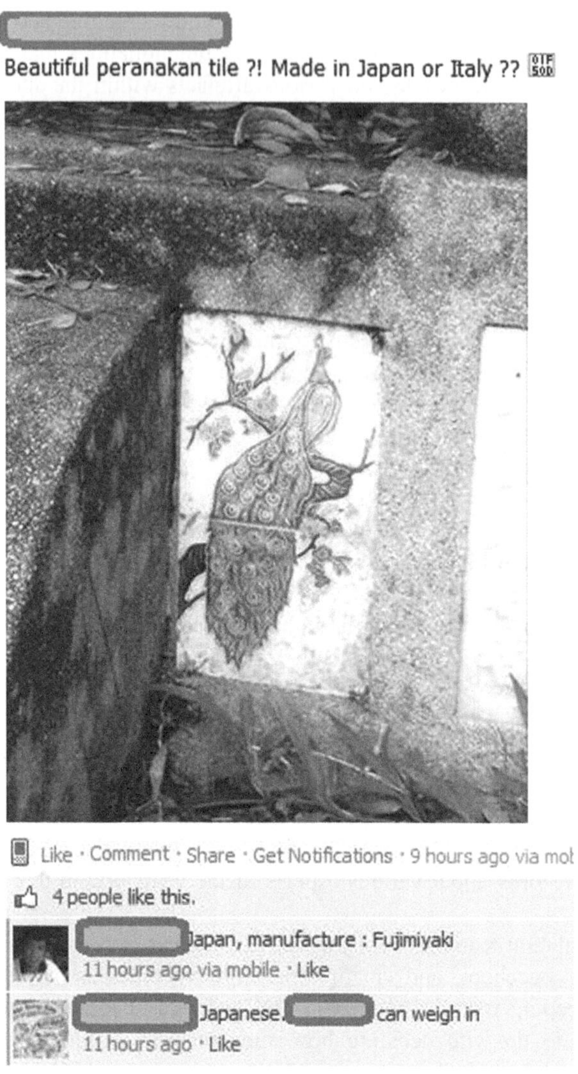

Figure 3. A record of participation in building knowledge.

has gained pace especially in the contemporary context, with the pressures of globalisation also quickly introducing changes in the ways people connect with each other, think about their heritage and clear lands (which may have cultural value) to make way for industrialisation. These changes culminate in the persistent need for documentation and archival work. Archiving in such contexts requires new facilitation skills, updated knowledge about the latest technologies and innovations, and constant sensitivities towards target users.

More than preservation

The discussion of this case study has so far illustrated two points. The first lies in how doing documentation in the field requires a cultural approach to both designing computing interventions and archival practices. The second is how the very practices of documenting, technological development and archiving may potentially shape cultural practices in the long run. Understanding that both points are recursive and dialogical is imperative to understanding the convergence of cultural systems (such as the one mentioned in this paper) with sociocultural practices. In other words, designing cultural systems with the sociocultural practices in mind can shape the very same sociocultural practices and, in the long run, lead to the sustainability of both the documentation and archival practices involved, and the technologies in use.

At this point, two factors are imminent which could raise important issues that should be considered in current and future scholarly work. The first is associated with the growing body of work on the digital archiving and preservation of cultural artefacts. Cultural institutions, government and international agencies, academics and technical enterprises alike have been concerned with the potential and challenges posed by digital preservation. Digital preservation, we argue, is not and should not be seen as a one-off activity. It should rather be an ongoing activity that is part of cultural practice. Additionally, the recognition that social systems (such as the BBC cultural system) are shaped by, and shape, cultural practices[11] suggests that the cultural system will contribute a certain trajectory in changes to the cultural practices surrounding Bukit Brown Cemetery. In other words, even as important cultural content is preserved via documentation and archival practices, it promotes ongoing use and accumulation of content which can come directly from users. In the long run, it provides a mechanism to ensure that digital preservation is a process rather than a one-off event.

The second and somewhat related proposition suggests that the system of participatory archives promotes and facilitates an active citizenry, a long-term effect which can only be observed over time. The convergence of multi-disciplinary practices in documentation, computing and archival work, loosely bound together via a structure of user participation, is representative of the function of remembering and collecting (a dialogical relationship) they share in common. In recent years the trend of convergence has been observed and discussed inter-institutions, among libraries, museums and archives,[12] but not as much has been said of how convergence is happening intra-institutions.

The case of Bukit Brown Cemetery's documentation project demonstrates how convergence may happen within each discipline: borrowing from the concept of the participatory archive, the scope of documentation is expanded to include records of participation, designing computing interventions with cultural inputs from documented information and users, and the examination of how archival requirements may be used to inform computing design and documentation work. While such convergence points to immediate benefits, such as greater innovation, information professionals acquiring diverse competencies, and collaboration at a greater intensity and velocity, Robinson cautions that practices should not be oversimplified for the sake of drawing parallels, and points of integration must be heeded (although her essay was based on memory institutions such as libraries, museums and archives). The use of technologies to facilitate collaboration must also be closely examined.

Conclusion

As both supposedly disinterested scholars assisting in the official documentation team in providing a more structured and technologised archival process, and ordinary citizens concerned with its demolition, the BBC project has posed a substantial affective challenge to the authors. Since the announcement of the planned development of the highway, the interest shown by the state, academia and the community has combined in an exercise seeking to document the site's inevitable disappearance, and in re-enchanting the site as a meaningful place worthy of preservation. For the government, the archival project has been one of reiterating its position on its cultural sensitivity to the heritage of BBC even if its physical existence could not be guaranteed. In contrast, for the docu-tivists, their efforts have focused on turning BBC into a heritage park that will serve as a cultural resource in which the original material culture of the tombstones has been technologically networked with a broader knowledge base.

For both authors, the BBC documentation project has emphasised missions to advocate for and exhibit archival records in new ways, as well as partnering with the docu-tivists to create meanings out of collections of records. Along with these functions comes an intricate understanding of the technologies creating the records. While Facebook is a great tool for facilitating social interactions and exchange of knowledge within the community, it is limited in terms of helping users reflect on the meanings of the records being created using the platform. Likewise for the augmented reality application, even though it is useful as a tool to monitor actual behaviour and interactions on site. As academics with backgrounds in social informatics, museum work and participatory archives, we were provided with an opportunity where archivists could pursue outcomes and missions of outreach and advocacy on a much greater scale than other archival projects.

The paper has presented the case of Bukit Brown Cemetery, a site at the brink of partial disappearance due to immediate and future development plans. The erosion of the physical landscape is not the only aspect of this cultural heritage that is at risk – more importantly, the sociocultural practices as well as community ties to the land are also threatened. With this context in mind, the documentation team designed and developed a project that would address the imminent challenges of disappearing cultural records, and also studied, as well as designed, technological interventions to promote cultural engagement. Such cultural engagement is further enhanced by the building of participatory archives within the project. In this discussion we have also reflected on the expanded role of the archivist, as well as what we observe as intra-disciplinary convergence in the case under study.

The eventual archive, although still a work in progress, is already rich with inputs and materials in various formats (images, text, audio recordings, videos), painstakingly generated by volunteers. At the same time pages on Facebook function as a vehicle for crowdsourcing inputs, and prove to be useful especially when information is not available from official sources for various reasons. For instance, some graves have been unattended for so long that it is unclear where to find useful records about the pioneers buried there. In other cases, significant records have been lost because so many generations have passed. We recognise that three important types of records need to be captured: 1) documents of graves as well as intangible records of social practices and memories associated with the graves, 2) user-generated information about various elements found within the site (see Figure 3 above for an example) and 3) salient records of how the Brownies have participated in making meanings about BBC using social media and other platforms.

The enriched archive could also potentially function as a source for the state to understand the heritage value of what will be lost to society. Through its meticulous detail the archive may make the loss more bearable when the site is developed as planned. This situation has posed challenges to both the state and the documentation team, as community stakeholders have criticised the documentation and archiving efforts as merely providing an excuse to continue the development plans for the area. Archivists engaged in these documentation projects will continue to have to deal with such challenges when working in wildly contested sites.

On the other hand, the archive may also provide an opportunity for archivists to become advocates for heritage preservation. By understanding the value of the archive, what is involved in building the archive and the interests of various stakeholders, the archivist helps to shape what is preserved and how this is preserved in the name of a given society as its heritage. Collaborations between stakeholders can be made possible with the common pursuit of heritage preservation, and the archivist is in a position to understand how that is possible by seeing the contextual connections within the archive.

The end goal, however, should not simply be an enriched archive. The process of participatory archiving and working in a multi-disciplinary documentation team provides opportunities to inform the community as well as other scholars and researchers. As demonstrated in the Bukit Brown Cemetery case, archivists have the opportunity to influence civic engagement and strengthen the ties within communities.

Acknowledgement

The authors would like to thank Dr Sebastian Gurciullo for his valuable time, inputs and comments which were most instrumental in improving the paper.

Notes

1. Serene Tan, 'My Father's Dream Fulfilled', *All Things Bukit Brown: Heritage.Habitat.History*, available at <*http://bukitbrown.com/main/?cat=88*>, accessed 8 February 2014.
2. 'Bukit Brown', *World Monuments Fund: Current Watch Site*, available at <*http://www.wmf.org/project/bukit-brown*>, accessed 2 January 2014.
3. E Wright, 'Rhetorical Spaces in Memorial Places: The Cemetery as a Rhetorical Memory Place/Space', *Rhetorical Society Quarterly*, vol. 35, no. 4, 2005, pp. 51–81.
4. A Giddens, *The Consequences of Modernity*, Stanford University Press, Chicago, 1990.
5. Social media can be seen as shaping both extensional and intensional transformations. It can move an individual out of his or her locale into the virtual sphere, where new and unexpected social relationships and interactions are to be expected. Yet at the same time the use of social media can also contribute to transformations in the individual's sense-making, desires, goals and purposes, and reflective meanings on life.
6. 'Bukit Brown', accessed 30 January 2014.
7. Urban Redevelopment Authority, 'LTA Finalises Alignment of New Road Across Bukit Brown', 19 March 2012, available at <*http://www.ura.gov.sg/pr/text/2012/pr12-26.html*>, accessed 31 January 2014.
8. Bukit Brown, 'iBBC – Tech Tombs', available at <*http://bukitbrown.com/main/?p=6096*>, accessed 31 January 2014.
9. I Huvila, 'Participatory Archive: Towards Decentralised Curation, Radical User Orientation, and Broader Contextualisation of Records Management', *Archival Science*, vol. 8, no. 1, 2008, pp. 15–36.
10. L Duranti, 'The Concept of Appraisal and Archival Theory', *American Archivist*, vol. 57, no. 2, Spring 1994, pp. 328–44.
11. WJ Orlikowski and D Robey, 'Information Technology and the Structuring of Organizations', *Information Systems Research*, vol. 2, no. 2, 1991, pp. 143–69.
12. R VanderBerg, 'Converging Libraries, Archives and Museums: Overcoming Distinctions, but for What Gain?', *Archives and Manuscripts*, vol. 40, no. 3, 2012, pp. 136–46. H Robinson, 'Remembering Things Differently: Museums, Libraries and Archives as Memory Institutions and the Implications for Convergence', *Museum Management and Curatorship*, vol. 27, no. 4, 2012, pp. 413–29.

Index

Note: Page numbers in **bold** type refer to figures
Page numbers followed by 'n' refer to notes

For Product Safety Concerns and Information please contact our EU representative GPSR@taylorandfrancis.com Taylor & Francis Verlag GmbH, Kaufingerstraße 24, 80331 München, Germany